Right and Wrong

Gerald Priestland is probably best known for his thirty-three years as a BBC correspondent. His posts ranged from 'Today in Parliament' to Delhi, Beirut and Washington, and ultimately Religious Affairs.

His talks 'Yours Faithfully' and 'Priestland's Progress' became national institutions and successful books.

On retiring from the BBC in 1982 he took up free-lance writing and broadcasting, including the two television series on which this book is based.

He was educated at Charterhouse and Oxford, where he was a pupil of Isaiah Berlin and Stuart Hampshire.

He is married to Sylvia Priestland, the printmaker, has four children and lives in North London and West Cornwall.

PRIESTLAND
Right and Wrong

—•◆•—

Gerald Priestland

in association with
Channel Four Television Company Limited

Collins
FOUNT PAPERBACKS

First published in Great Britain in 1983
by William Collins Sons & Co. Ltd, London
Published by Fount Paperbacks, London in 1984

Copyright © Gerald Priestland 1983

Made and printed in Great Britain
by William Collins Sons & Co. Ltd, Glasgow

Contents

Introduction   *page* 7

Chapter 1 And Make Me a Good
             Girl – Amen   10
       2   Arms and the Man   24
       3   The Violent Society   37
       4   God and Mammon   51
       5   Right Honourable Friends   66
       6   In the Family Way   82
       7   Publish and Be Damned   97
       8   The God Squad   112
       9   Enjoy, Enjoy!   129
      10   Blessed are the Poor   143
      11   Work or What?   159
      12   God Made the Land   176
      13   Whose Life in Whose Hands?   191

Further Reading   205

Introduction

I am not one of those who rejects the good things of life or believes there is no such thing as progress. But I think the spectacular progress made during the past hundred years on the material front has led us to neglect our spiritual natures. Man does not live by bread alone, nor by cars, television or annual wage increases. When he behaves as if he did, an aching void is left within him and he must find something to fill it. If religion is discredited, he will be drawn to social, political or economic ideals.

Yet these, too, fail to satisfy because they are all too human and lead back once more to material values. Neither technology nor politics nor economics has delivered the Good Life, nor can they.

In this crisis many people have been driven back to their latent sense of God. Too often they do not know what to do about it because they find – or imagine – the Church to be irrelevant to their lives in the world. I sympathise with them. Many more are aware of something which I believe depends upon God (though God is a great deal more), namely their conscience or moral sense.

I am not principally concerned in this book to argue the case for Christianity, though I believe in it and that will show. My purpose is to encourage people's confidence in their sense of right and wrong – to urge them to choose to choose. For I choose, therefore I am.

I do not claim any originality in this. I think I am only expressing a feeling which is already in the air. In recent years there has been a succession of 'great debates' on moral issues – abortion, euthanasia, nuclear weapons and power, the right to strike, blood sports, laboratory animals, aid to the Third World, the ecology, an endless list – which has clearly demonstrated the popular anxiety to discern what is right and not merely expedient.

But these debates have also revealed a widespread feeling of individual helplessness in the face of the systems in which people are caught up: systems ranging from the world economic order through nations, parties, administrations, unions and companies down to schools, local communities and groups of friends. People feel they ought to be making choices but are powerless to do so. Even if they made them, what impact would it have upon impersonal structures which are constantly becoming bigger and better organised?

We have to resist such defeatism if we are to remain human beings; though the choices before us are neither simple to make nor easy to execute. In the two television series upon which this book is based I selected various fields of human activity – for example, business, politics, the mass media – and discussed not only what the principles of right and wrong might be, but the difficulties of putting them into practice. (I have followed the general form of the television scripts, with some development and expansion.)

One reason why there are no simple answers is that when a moral problem is felt, that is usually a sure sign that two or more issues are in conflict. It is almost impossible to find the right solution to one without committing an offence against another. It is a sign of the moral person that he or she is aware of this but does not make it an excuse for inaction.

Television is a difficult medium in which to handle abstract ideas, but to a communicator it offers the irresistible chance to interest viewers who might not normally consider such ideas. At least they may be sufficiently intrigued by one's fleeting messages to want to ponder them at leisure on the printed page. I am grateful, therefore, to my director Alan Ravenscroft; to our researcher, Olave Snelling; to John Mills, our cameraman; and to the entire TVS crew for their tolerance, skill and companionship. My thanks also to Lord Hailsham, Sir William Rees-Mogg, Tony Benn, Sydney Bailey and many other friends who granted me time to discuss the issues, though none of them should be held responsible for what I made of it all.

Book and television alike would have been impossible without the support of John Ranelagh of Channel 4 and Angus Wright of TVS at Southampton. The televised images have gone with the wind, but these words remain a while longer in thanks to them.

CHAPTER ONE

And Make Me a Good Girl – Amen

'You ought to be ashamed of yourself!'

I have totally forgotten what dreadful offence I had committed, there in the dormitory of Winchester House School, Brackley, in the year of Our Lord 1935. It was probably something to do with nudity. But that was almost fifty years ago and the thundrous arrival of Miss Ash – with her coal black wig, sallow skin and purple bosom – has driven everything else from my memory, save that terrible curse that I ought to be ashamed of myself.

I had, in fact, heard the words before: once from my nursery maid at home, when I had piddled from under one leg of my shorts instead of through the flies; and often from the lips of Mr Growser, resident curmudgeon of Toytown, in the *Children's Hour* broadcasts. Neither was to be taken seriously. But Miss Ash was the Day of Judgment in bombazine. There was no appeal from her wrath, and I cringed before it, the most miserable of sinners.

Part of my punishment was to kneel beside my bed and pray out loud for forgiveness. The only prayer I could remember had been taught me by that nursery maid – a girl from Durham, called Christine – and I copied her so slavishly that, to the enduring scorn of Miss Ash, I finished up 'And make me a good girl – Amen'. Alone in my darkness and misery, I began to wrestle with the problem that has exercised me ever since: Why ought I to be ashamed of myself? What could it possibly mean?

I could see I had done something that adults did not like,

and experience taught me that life was happier if one did not displease the powerful. It was fairly pointless to argue about why they were displeased at the sight of a seven-year-old skipping about naked. But as I grew older I became more and more intrigued with the principles behind the words of Miss Ash. In effect they had been an order to stop doing something and take my punishment for it. But they would still have meant something if I had carried on unpunished – more, even, than 'I do not like what you are doing'. It was another fourteen years before I came to the conclusion that Miss Ash was saying something like 'If you were me, you would not behave like that' – and even that is not the end of it. What are these orders that nobody gives, these crimes that injure nobody, these punishments that leave no mark?

Moral Philosophy – which is the academic name for all this – was part of my course at Oxford. 'Have you *read* any moral philosophy?' asked my New College tutor, at my first session with him. 'Lots of C. S. Lewis', I said confidently. He winced, as if in pain: 'Mr Lewis is hardly a philosopher.'

Oxford philosophy in those days meant Mr A. J. Ayer, Mr Stuart Hampshire and company, and was much concerned with whether what people said actually meant anything at all, and what tests one could apply to see whether it was true. In this atmosphere, the consensus was that statements about morals were meaningless, since there was no way of measuring or verifying them and they did not proceed from pure logic. The best defence one could put up for them was that people obstinately went on saying things like right and wrong, moral and immoral, ought and ought not *as if* they meant something; and surely such people were not just idiots talking Jabberwocky?

I was not, at that time, a very serious Christian. Spiritually, I was 'just resting' after successive phases of public school anglicanism and militant atheism. So I played philosophical word-games for their own sake and emerged with the discovery that 'morally prescriptive statements are really conditional descriptive statements' – that is to say, 'You ought to be ashamed of yourself really means that if you were me you *would* feel ashamed of yourself'. Which still leaves a lot of questions unanswered, notably *Why?*

I scarcely returned to them for the next thirty years. That I did so was partly the result of advancing age, partly of a mental crisis resolved by psychiatry, partly of whatever will of the Spirit called me into religious journalism. It simply became impossible to live in the two worlds of religion and current affairs without demanding to know how they could occupy the same universe sometimes so closely together and sometimes so far apart. And so, at the invitation of a television company, I came back to moral philosophy knowing myself to be the most abject of amateurs but determined – this time – to wrestle some answers from it.

It seemed a good idea to return to Oxford. Lolling in a punt on the River Cherwell, I immediately began to have moral misgivings. Quite apart from whether my ethical pilgrimage would satisfy the experts, was it right to display it on television, that extravagant opiate of the masses, that trivial substitute for useful activity? Would I not be better employed designing packages, teaching immigrant children, servicing cars, milking cows or caring for geriatric cases, like the other members of my family; or like my friend Roger, who actually gave up scribbling and broadcasting to join the Department of Health and Social Security? These questions bothered me to such an extent that I could make a living out of bothering. And that bothered me, too.

Yet there was no physical pain involved. I was not doing anything illegal by lounging in my punt, and nobody was going to hit me or send me to prison for it. The fact that I was actually going to get paid for doing it suggested that, after all, I was doing something useful – or at any rate, something that somebody wanted to buy. Perhaps it was not wrong of me. Perhaps it was something I ought to be doing, something with which my conscience could be at peace.

And there were those extraordinary words again – *wrong, ought, conscience*. My hand, trailing in the water, could have told you whether it was hot or cold. Had you been there, your hand could have told you the same: we would almost certainly have agreed on it. But we might often differ as to what is right or wrong. A deed can even be legal and yet, in many eyes, wrong. And while I can show you the hand that judges the temperature of the water, I cannot show you my conscience or write out a chemical formula for rectitude. Is it possible that right and wrong do not actually exist – that we have been brainwashed into thinking they do – or that they are really something else? Alternatively, perhaps they are so important and self-evident that I am playing a dangerous game by picking at them.

My fantasy on the Cherwell was still in the old Oxford tradition of playing word-games instead of laying down the law. But the games, like those on the playing-fields of Eton where Waterloo was won, are more serious than may appear. The ideas of today's philosophers are passed on to tomorrow's teachers, politicians and writers to become the taken-for-granted beliefs of ordinary people the day after. And it is important to use words carefully, because if we cannot talk to each other effectively, we end up hitting each other. Throw words about carelessly, as Hitler did, and people eventually die for them. Besides, most of us use words to think with, and if we are not in control of them we lose control of our thinking, and somebody else may run away with our minds.

As my disgrace before Miss Ash reveals, a great deal of moral talk has to do with social behaviour and our relations with other people. When people say 'You ought to do that' they are implying 'You are expected to do that: if you were a completely recognisable member of the team I belong to you *would* do that'. This raises some interesting questions about how you get recognised as belonging to a certain team or group, class or society: about 'the sort of person you are or present yourself as being. It suggests a possible conflict between how others see you and expect you to behave, and how you see yourself. But for the moment, what matters is what is expected. Human beings like the people around them to behave predictably.

We dislike unpredictability, disorder and chaos because they mean a life full of stress and threats and danger. The commerce of life becomes impossible if people do not behave as they are expected to do by those with whom they must interact. So one purpose of the moral order is to have order at all.

I have to thank my friend Professor J. P. Lachmann – a Cambridge scientist who happens also to be a bee-keeper – for pointing out a possible evolutionary reason for this[1]. He argues that unlike bees, whose behaviour depends almost entirely on their genetic inheritance, human beings are subject to a much more rapid kind of evolution, *cultural* evolution. In this, behaviour is passed on and modified not by the slow shuffling of genes but by the transmission of information, using the senses, language and writing. It is this cultural evolution, rather than the genetic variety, which has enabled mankind to advance from the Stone Age to the Silicon Chip Age in a mere four hundred generations. By using language to pass on information, each generation has been able to instruct its successors in what kind of behaviour is best adapted to survival in the circumstances. Professor Lachmann sees religion as primarily a way of prescribing and imposing such systems of behaviour. This leads him to conclude that, on the one hand, it is dangerous

---

[1] 'Why Religions? An Evolutionary View of the Behaviour of Bees and Men', *The Cambridge Review*, 28th January 1983

to abandon a well-tried religious system for an experimental novelty, while, on the other, there is little future for a religion which risks the impoverishment of its followers by banning birth-control.

I cannot, myself, see Lachmann's thesis as a threat to God, since I see no reason why God should act other than 'scientifically'. And if moral behaviour is evolutionarily adaptive behaviour, beneficial to our survival, so much the better. No believer in God should expect otherwise.

Nevertheless, I do not think religion is only to do with the prescribing and enforcing of moral behaviour, and nor does Lachmann, who writes of 'other elements of the religion', by which he means various dogmas, threats and superstitions. The trouble is, Lachmann limits himself by taking Dr Johnson's enlightened definition of religion as 'Virtue, as founded upon reverence for God and expectation of future rewards and punishments'. Theologically, this is quaint. To me, at least, virtue is an unconscious by-product of the knowing of God, and it is that knowing, experience, understanding which religion is really about.

So we return from our visit to the bees with the impression that order is not the whole story, though it is a very important part of it. Almost any system which enables us to predict how people will treat one another is better than none at all, and to that extent will be deemed right.

But surely, if right and wrong are beneficial there should be little argument about morality? Perhaps the arguments arise from the fact that right and wrong are not absolute but variable. According to a 1981 Gallup Survey[2] two-thirds of the British consider there are no absolute guidelines to good and evil and that these have to be judged according to circumstances.

Undoubtedly the circumstances that throw up our moral conflicts do change. Some of the issues that trouble us today, like birth-control, nuclear power, medical control

[2] *European Values – Summary Results 1981* Social Surveys (Gallup Poll)

over life, did not exist for mediaeval Oxford. Almost all moral philosophers would agree there are greater and lesser goods and evils. But that there are some absolutes to be aspired to, standards of right and wrong which are unchanging, is a very ancient tradition indeed. It is certainly the tradition of the Christian Church, which is still deep in the moral thinking of our culture.

To the Greeks and Romans, the four cardinal virtues were prudence, temperance, fortitude and justice. These are good, soldierly qualities and their noblest product was probably Stoicism, with its devotion to reason, duty and self-control and its courageous acceptance of whatever fate might bring. In many ways, Stoicism remains the natural religion of the better type of English public school boy. It is not, however, particularly Christian, and it lacked the humanity to win a popular following.

To the classical virtues, Christians added the Pauline trio of faith, hope and charity – all a bit wet by Stoic standards. Since the mediaeval Church also identified seven deadly sins – pride, covetousness, lust, envy, gluttony, anger and sloth – it follows that their opposites, like humility, chastity and industriousness, were virtues. Today, if you were to ask the average person what qualities they admired, they would probably list values like kindness, honesty and fairness. The British are traditionally keen on fairness: "tisn't fair!' is the age-old cry of the resentful British worker – and of the British child. It is a cry for justice, for order and no queue-jumping. The difficulty is, it conflicts with the virtue of individual freedom. How two virtues, each supposed to be morally good in itself, can conflict with one another is one of the fundamental problems of ethics; indeed, it is one of two main reasons for the existence of such problems at all.

The first reason is the difficulty of finding the will to do what we know we *should* do: the strength and motivation to follow our judgment with action. The lack of such will can lead to the turning of blind eyes and the spinning of elaborate excuses. The second cause of problems is the fact that many, if not most, moral dilemmas are not single issues but multiple ones. It is easy enough to know that I should not steal a loaf of bread. But if I am penniless and my child is starving – what takes precedence? On a more sophisticated level, if the Russians are about to invade Germany, do I drop the bomb on them or sacrifice the liberty of the Germans? Any of these questions by itself would be simple enough to answer; it is the conflicts and connections between them that make the agony; for the grading and comparing of goods and evils cannot be quantified, often involve guesswork about consequences.

The basic moral values have been around for much longer than the Christian religion, and the Church has always recognised 'natural morality' as implicit in human nature. In almost any race and culture you will find certain standards – the telling of truth and keeping of promises, some kind of sexual discipline, respect for human life and private property – insisted upon to varying degrees: all justifiable for evolutionary reasons.

There is little outside that category in the Ten Commandments. After the first three (no other gods, no blasphemy or sabbath-breaking) the remaining seven are about social order and property. They are the kind of rules that any reasonable secular club might draw up to avoid quarrelling among its members. But the Commandments are solemnly presented as part of a contract or Covenant with Jehovah: God undertaking to support Israel on condition that Israel observes His Law. What this does is to give divine authority to the civil order and to make any breach of it tantamount to blasphemy. Israel is to obey the Law not just because it is sensible and convenient (in which case, man might reasonably alter it to suit the circumstances) but because it is the will of God. Jehovah is a reliable God who does not break His promises. He will not withdraw His favours provided Israel does not withdraw its obedience. Thus, almost any national disaster is seen as a punishment, and the link between morality and the supernatural is forged fast.

To the humanist this may appear a piece of priestly blackmail, so I will make the word 'God' disappear for a while. After all, you do not have to believe in a personal God to be a thoroughly decent citizen, as honest, kind and loved by all as any devout churchgoer.

There goes a pretty girl. It would be nice to slip an arm round her waist and give her breast a squeeze – and why not, since no thunderbolt will strike me dead, and I shan't go to hell when I die? Yet I don't do it, despite the chances of getting away with it, because something tells me it is wrong. Quite apart from involved arguments about human dignity and equality, if I really were the sort of person I like to think I am, I would *not* do it. And so I don't. I remain the sort of person I hoped I was, which pleases me. In a word, it is my conscience.

But is not conscience, in the end, just the voice of my parents (and the terrible Miss Ash), programmed into my mind like a computer and triggered off by the situations I run into ? You can see it happening with any small child, who steals and lies and covets spontaneously, until he learns that such behaviour makes his parents cross, risking the loss of their love. Nevertheless, wrong-doing has its satisfactions, too, in the short run. Quite early on in life, there are agonising calculations to be made.

But in practical terms we cannot go through life like little Hamlets making agonising calculations at every step. The decisions come at you all the time, and you have to rely on quick, built-in reactions. Human beings, however, have enormously complex brains and we seem to take almost twenty years to reach the point of responsible independence. Indeed, I am not sure whether the age of moral maturity is not fifty or sixty – which is less silly than it

sounds, when you remark how the statistics for mis-
behaviour fall off with middle age.

Parents and teachers can imagine they are programming
their children's consciences successfully – or 'bringing them
up nicely' as it is called – until the dreaded teenage strikes,
and everything falls at the mercy of the sex hormones and
the herd instinct. At the root of it all lies the question: What
sort of person am I? It is the search for a personal order, an
identity, a true nature freely chosen.

The teenage personality reshuffle seldom ends up as
badly as parents fear; for it is very hard to shake off a past
that has been with you since birth. It is tempting to conclude from this that we are totally moulded by our heredity
and environment, and that free will is an illusion.

But beware reductionism – the urge to oversimplify
enormously complex issues by saying they are 'really only'
something else. Conscience is not really only the result of
our childhood, any more than music is really only an echo
from the womb or God really only the dream of a grand-
father in the skies.

The longing for simple answers leads some people to
maintain that the moral key to everything can be found in
the Bible. But I do not find the Bible at all simple, and I do
not see how you can look up pacifism or birth-control or
nuclear power in it and find a simple answer there.

Indeed, I do not know of any handbook of morals to be
used like a motor-car manual – although enough has been
written on the subject to build a rather stuffy four-
bedroomed house. People have argued that the Good lies in
finding the greatest happiness of the greatest number,
which I suppose is what democratic governments are trying
to do most of the time. But happiness *when* – immediately,
or in the long run? And how long? And, which is more
important, the happiness or the numbers? And is happiness
the same as pleasure?

Despite Marx's protestations, Marxist morality is a version of this approach. The greatest number is supposed to be the working class, and whatever is in the material interest of the workers ought to be right. Old-fashioned capitalist morality was a repressive device to secure the material interests — the happiness — of the ruling class and its lackeys. There is obviously something in this. We would find it impossible today to justify slavery, but generations of English, Spanish and American slave-owners went to church with comfortable consciences — and the connivance of St Paul.

So there is no doubt that morality is affected, and maybe perverted, by social and economic circumstances. You and I compromise our principles all the time. Yet why do we not go flat out for our own selfish interests? Is it only because we fear the law, or memories of our parents, or make elaborate calculations about the survival of the race? I think all of these enter into it. I do not think morality would be so powerful if it were not confirmed and enforced by factors like these. But it cannot explain why, sometimes, what we know we ought to do flies in the face of the law, horrifies our parents and outrages society.

Though we negotiate most of the day 'on automatic pilot', the fact is that at any time we can choose to reflect on what we are doing. We can contemplate behaving not as the sort of person we are expected to be, but as the sort of person we want to be. We want to conform to a new and – we believe – better order. We can choose. But the crucial thing is that, first of all, we must choose to choose. We must decide to come off automatic pilot, reflect about what we are doing, and be prepared to change our ways, even at the cost of being thought eccentric.

This is the classic moral decision and, thank goodness, it does not confront us very often. It requires an effort of will, of free will, for it is not enough for our conscience to sense what we ought to do: we have to persuade ourselves to do it, voluntarily, or it is no choice at all and we have merely defined ourselves as victims of circumstance.

I believe that we have to start with free will as a fact; that it is nonsense to pretend it does not exist. I choose, therefore I am; and I think those who are driven to doubt their free will are confused in three directions:

1) Nobody is one hundred per cent free. It would be intolerable as well as impossible for every moral decision to be taken from scratch. But there is a vital proportion – a casting vote – which we can control by choice.

2) There is a certain futility in contemplating the choices we 'might have made' had we asserted our wills. The past is done and cannot be revised. In that sense, it is determined for us.

3) A great deal of what we shall do is either predictable from where we are now or at the mercy of events we cannot foresee. But the former is not necessarily against our will, and the latter not necessarily without opportunities for choice. Some people who deny free will are really complaining that they lack the power to work miracles.

Perhaps conscience does resemble a computer: but who programmes it? Many sources. Our parents, our society, our companions; and we ourselves, and God, if we choose. If we choose, the programme can be overridden and revised.

The Catholic Church, widely accused of authoritarianism, acknowledges the supremacy of the individual conscience. But, it says, it must be an informed conscience, not one that is selfish, ignorant and pigheaded. It has to be properly instructed and maintained. It is possible for conscience to fall into disuse, become rusty, starved, covered with cobwebs. Simply not choosing to make moral choices – cruising along the line of least resistance – may be the obvious way through life, but it leads to moral decay and to the very disorder that society dreads. The living conscience requires constant exercise.

All of which sounds stern and a little pompous. Fortunately most of the things that exercise our conscience are everyday and commonsense. To a remarkable degree, moral behaviour means behaving reasonably: it is usually in our own best interest to do what is right. Unfortunately, we live in a society which has grown suspicious of too much verbalising and increasingly refuses to think logically.

But logic and reason cannot be the whole story. Heroism is not reasonable, nor is sacrifice, modesty, entering a monastery for a life of prayer or many other things which are still admired for their moral value. I come back to the question: What sort of person do I think I am?

It is sometimes argued that the aim of life should be to realise our full potentials, to liberate, gratify and satisfy our reasonable desires. Before long, however, satisfying desires *fails* to satisfy; and if we all tried at once, there would be total disorder and the frustration of all desires. The religious person has always preferred the question: What sort of person am I meant to be by that outside power which I feel caring for me and for all humanity? That most men have always been aware of such a power remains a fact. They usually call it God, and they find it to be the one thing that makes sense of life; for it is the one thing they encounter both in life and above it. If you ask why life should make sense at all, I can only say that no one I have ever watched acted as if life were wholly absurd.

We must be able to deny and reject the idea of God. The same free will that grants us the choice of right or wrong *must* grant us God or No God. I have said that religion – the knowing of God – is far more than a code of morals. But if there is a God who creates us, doing right must involve following His design for our nature; and doing wrong must involve going astray from that design. Since part of the design is evidently that we live together socially and reproduce ourselves, it is small wonder that much of what is right turns out to be good citizenship. Yet another part of the design is very mysterious, though.

If there is a God with designs for us, it would be outrageous if He gave us no idea of what they are. Religious people are convinced that He does, within our capacity to grasp them and according to our willingness to look and listen for them. Christians believe that God communicates through the scriptures, through history, through prophets and sacraments and – if we are attentive – through our very consciences.

At its deepest level, conscience is programmed by God, who has set in it the code for our true nature. Yet because of the gift of free will (without which we would be mere puppets) we have received the right to think we know better; the right to fall and to sin. And this we are bound to do, as we know perfectly well. We know that we have acted, and shall act, contrary to our own best interests and the interests of those to whom we are bound in love and duty; and we know that our failure is due to the fact that we have not chosen to choose.

The special thing about the Christian faith is that it enables us to live with this failure, without cynicism or despair. It offers us forgiveness – the continuing sense of our own worth – and the strength to attempt the impossible once more. Even as we fail, we can (as the song puts it) pick ourselves up, dust ourselves off, and start right over again. There are other ways of fighting the battle, some of them worthy of our highest respect; but there is none other, I think, that speaks so understandingly to human nature.

CHAPTER TWO

Arms and the Man

Of all the fields for human moral choice none is harder to negotiate than the battlefield. For it is literally a matter of life and death and it is littered with concepts like honour, courage, patriotism and sacrifice which are not very amenable to logical argument. It is also swept by the crosswinds of politics and obscured by clouds of rhetoric.

Of all the films that we made exploring questions of right and wrong in action, the one dealing with war was the most difficult to arrange. I began by writing my script; and I hope the reader will agree, by the end of this chapter, that although I could not renounce my personal vocation to pacifism I dealt fairly with those who feel otherwise. Certainly the soldiers to whom we showed the script acknowledged that and declared themselves happy to cooperate in filming it. It was when the script was referred back to the civil servants and their political masters that resistance set in. Could the British Army be allowed to associate itself with a film that challenged not only government policy but its own reason for being? 'First the CND, then the churches, and now you!' expostulated one official; and then pointed out phrase after phrase which, he feared, were going to send his superiors 'up the wall'.

We pointed out that, according to the soldiers, the army's main reason for being was to defend our liberties, including the liberty to say things like that. We declined to alter any of the offending remarks, and as weeks passed without a decision either way from the Department of Defence, we began to make arrangements to film the script abroad – on the battlefields of World War I.

It is just possible that the authorities began to have bad dreams of headlines about THE FILM THEY TRIED TO GAG; or that they came round to my own belief that the influence of television is grossly overrated anyway. A nobler explanation would be that British freedom of speech won the day; for much to the credit of all concerned our permission came through with less than a week to spare, and we deployed our crew over Sandhurst, the military cemetery at Brookwood and the ranges of Salisbury Plain, to be welcomed on every occasion as if we had been making a recruiting film. The only concession we made, at our own suggestion, was a closing caption thanking the Army units concerned for defending our right to say what we did. And that I repeat here.

I have covered four wars in my time as a reporter – including Vietnam – but except as a Home Guard I have never been in any position to fire a shot at an enemy. So I still find it curious that an act of killing which could have me convicted of murder in one set of circumstances, could win me a medal in another. O my enemy, you too loved your wife and children! Like me, you were a sort of Christian, you adored your native countryside and found comfort in the music of Bach. Why should I be decorated because my government believes your government is in the wrong, as passionately (no doubt) as your government believes mine is? Apparently the law against killing is suspended when there is no other way of self-preservation. Life, it is claimed, cannot be expected to tolerate its own destruction; though that argument looks open to exceptions.

If one or the other of two antagonists is going to be destroyed, why should not *I* volunteer to be the loser? There are such people, and you might say Jesus was one. He could have resisted, but He chose to fight by surrendering. Some people find that so moving and powerful an example that they aspire to follow it.

As far as we know, there has always been war, and there are few signs in the wind that it will not always be so. Yet cannibalism is a thing of the past, and human sacrifice and slavery, and the subjugation of women seems to be on the way out. Even soldiers nowadays insist that they arm with a view to making war impossible, rather than to enforce the will of the state. If they are sincere about this (as the best undoubtedly are) there must be an underlying acknowledgement that their weapons *ought not* to be used. We must be able to imagine a world in which they *would not* be used – if only those beastly foreigners did not cheat on the rules which *we* always observe. For we, of course, behave better.

It is the wisdom of the ages that unless a community believes it is morally right, it will go to pieces. Those in authority get worried about movements which insist that their own country is sometimes wrong, because authority fears that unless the other side also entertains such doubts, the one that does entertain them will be weakened. It would, indeed, be intolerable to belong to a country which you knew to be acting wickedly; so most governments spend much time convincing their peoples they are right. One way a nation purges itself of being caught in the wrong is to blame the government and get rid of it. Though this is sometimes easier said than done.

For the instruments of force are not employed solely to preserve the nation against outsiders. In the eyes of government, they may be necessary to protect the nation from part of itself. Just as individuals will go to almost any length to survive, so governments are tempted to use force to stay in power – to avoid admitting moral bankruptcy and so committing suicide. No government actually believes itself to be wicked and repressive: however undemocratic it may be, it persuades itself that it represents the true interests of the nation, and it believes it is morally right to use force when people are too stupid or misled to see that. The British are lucky to have evolved a society where that kind of thinking is unfashionable. But it was not always so, and with no entrenched constitution of absolute rights it is always possible for government by force to return to Britain. The appeal to firm, straightforward discipline with no clever answering back will always get a round of applause.

Nevertheless, human beings desire to be moral creatures: hardly anyone goes about grabbing things on the simple basis that might is right. When it draws the sword or in any way forces people to do something, a government will seek to justify itself morally in one of two ways: either the action makes for the greatest good of the greatest number, or it is necessary for law and order (which amounts to the same thing). As we have seen, unpredictability is dangerous and exhausting, and if necessary governments will compel people to behave predictably.

It is the same in the society of nations. If one country behaves in a disorderly, unpredictable way, other countries feel morally justified in trying to bring it to heel. Unpredictability, in each other's terms, is the greatest cause of world tension and ultimately of war. Hence the attempt to impose logic, order and understanding through the United Nations and, before it, the League.

Few nations nowadays pretend that war is fun, a manly virtue for its own sake, or a legitimate way of acquiring attractive property. It can never have been much fun in the Dark Ages, hacking away face to face with your opponent; but the bloodbath of the First World War and the continuing impact of the war correspondent seem to have made Anglo-Saxon generals, at any rate, a great deal more tender about sacrificing their soldiers in hecatombs.

But whatever scruples may have stirred, war is still alive and flourishing throughout the globe. Including terrorist campaigns and tribal revolts, there were more than thirty going on in January 1983. Seeing that those who begin such outbreaks usually fail to secure their objects – or achieve something quite different from what they had hoped for – war is not even an efficient method of getting what you want. And the more complex war becomes (today it is like setting up and running an entire economy) the harder it is to control. Perhaps the most powerful argument for peace at any price is that nobody can predict where conflict is going to lead. It is not quite true that war settles nothing: the real catastrophe is that it creates worse problems than it solves. We begin by trying to eject Hitler from Poland, and end up dropping the atom bomb on Japan and relinquishing most of Eastern Europe to Stalin.

Yet honourable men are still prepared to lay down their lives, because they say it is unthinkable that we should not resist what we know to be wrong. War is the last resort of virtue. For evil to triumph, it is only necessary that good men should do nothing.

It might appear that, for the good man, the worst thing he could do was to take the life of his fellow man. 'Thou shalt not kill'. Or is it 'Thou shalt not commit murder'? For having received the Ten Commandments, the children of Israel marched off and committed nothing short of genocide upon the Midianites, with the full approval of Jehovah. And the same went for the Hittites and the Amorites, the Canaanites and the Perizzites, the Hivites and the Jebusites (see Deuteronomy, Chapter 20).

But that was before Christ; and for the Christian, surely, it must be a kind of sacrilege to destroy a brother or sister made in the image of God. Yet Christians do kill each other in battle, with good conscience and with chaplains in support on both sides.

Now, pacifists come in various grades and I am not, myself, the variety which will have nothing whatever to do with war. I would sooner our soldiers were shepherded as Christians than abandoned as lost souls; and once peace had broken down, I would be ready to carry one end of a stretcher and do what I could to succour the casualties. I am not one of those who regards the soldier as an evil man. Contemplating the armed forces of Britain, I find it impossible not to be generally proud of them: over the past century and more, they have never sought to rule us, only to serve us. They sum up the sort of people we like to think we are: not brutal robots, but reasonable, team-spirited and kindly individuals, doing what has to be done without savagery.

But the soldier kills and I (I hope) cannot, though I can see a very nasty problem in whether I should endanger my comrades by refusing to do so. What right has the individual to say that his isolated view of what is right must take precedence over that of the community on which he depends for so much?

If such a right does *not* exist, then there is no morality – only the majority vote. In Britain both the Church and the State do recognise the claims of conscientious objection; though, again, it must be an informed conscience, prepared to suffer the consequences of being odd man out, and not selfish cowardice. Refusing to fight is neither popular nor easy. It is hardly even natural; though pacifists always encounter less hostility among soldiers at the front than they do among those civilians who are furthest from the fighting.

It is not easy, in particular, to preserve a pacifist stance in the face of the war against Hitler. For resistance worked, did it not? Evil was crushed and right triumphed, and what alternative that would have worked can the pacifist suggest? Not to resist evil sounds like an open licence for piracy. War itself may be evil. But we are all fallen, sinful men and the world we have made often presents nothing better than the lesser of two evils. Is not freedom a clear Christian good, for which it may be worth sacrificing life itself? Does not good always have to be brought forth in pain?

I find that very persuasive, and in a curious way I could

not be a pacifist if there were any chance of pacifism imposing itself on people who sincerely felt like that. Pacifism will certainly not work until most people everywhere believe in it as firmly as they now believe (mistakenly, I think) that war works. The obligation upon pacifists to convince their fellow men, especially in communist lands and in countries still enforcing conscription, seems to me far more important than direct action against nuclear bases.

Much was heard during the Falklands campaign of the Doctrine of the Just War: that concept of the mediaeval Church which sought to limit war by various standards. The cause must be just, force must be the last resort, there must be reasonable hope of success, the means proportionate to the end, civilians to be immune from hostilities and so forth – all of which Britain would claim to have respected. As modern warfare goes, the Falklands campaign was controlled and humane, partly by skill and not a little by luck. The international community, too, makes sporadic attempts to limit warfare by voting for ceasefires, dispatching peace-keeping forces, negotiating agreements on chemical and biological weapons and nibbling at the limitation of conventional and nuclear armaments. Is not this legalistic approach – rather than the hopeless prayer of pacifism – the more promising way ahead?

But we are no longer in the age of the dreadnought, the howitzer and the Flying Fortress. Over the past half century, the nature of war and the moral decisions raised by it *at every level* have been utterly transformed by three major developments. They are not just matters of degree, of old bangs made bigger, but of entry into a new world – alas, with the same old heads on our shoulders.

The first is the development and toleration, during World War II, of *total* warfare: war for men, women and children, regardless of where they are or what they are doing, how old or helpless they may be. The Doctrine of the Just War required noncombatants to be left alone – you did not massacre peasants or ravage the crops. But from about 1940 onwards, crops, factories and industrial workers have all been fair game. Inevitably, since if you bomb an arms centre from eighteen thousand feet you can hardly guarantee to hit only the workshops. Moreover, every able-bodied enemy subject is a potential conscript or arms-maker. So the allies incinerate Hamburg and Dresden, and the Germans wreck Liverpool and Coventry.

And with total war has come the absolute weapon: the hydrogen bomb in superfluity, described as a deterrent and yet never, apparently, enough of a deterrent for it to be unnecessary to make more. The argument goes that it has indeed deterred, since there has been no Great War between the major powers for almost forty years. There have, instead, been at least two medium-size conflicts between the powers or their nominees (Korea and Vietnam) and various other seizures of territory, none of which has been deterred in the least. As for World War III, it will be little comfort to think the bomb bought us forty years of peace if our children are destroyed on the fiftieth. Can we really gamble on the theory that, thanks to the bomb, the next war between super-powers will confine itself to a game of tactical ping-pong on the East German border? Or that we can stand a first strike, because our second strike will knock the Russians out? Unless those warheads are fraudulent, a day or two of them will leave little to choose between winner and loser. It is not going to be like rebuilding London after the blitz, and anyone with the power to hold off that kind of desolation is going to be in a different moral context from Mr Neville Chamberlain.

Finally there is the growth of sophisticated irregular warfare – terrorism, guerrilla campaigns, liberation movements, which have only a few years to go before they, too, move into the nuclear weapons age. Such movements invariably claim to have high moral reasons for adopting low immoral tactics. Usually they set themselves goals which are far beyond reasonable hope of attainment and, when authority refuses to give way, are driven to increasingly brutal gestures to make their impact. The end is invoked to justify the means. Atrocities are blamed upon governments 'for not granting our just demands', and since terrorism is extremely hard to deal with by conventional methods, governments are often dragged down to the terrorist level.

And so a hellish sophistry gains currency, with murders described as executions and burnt-out shops and homes described as targets. A whole literature has grown up to give respectability to the perversion. Worse still, there are international networks of training and finance. Brigandage is an ancient trade, but never before has it been systematically organised across frontiers. It is yet another example of a system developing its own impetus, regardless of any reasonable aims or morality.

Because of these three developments – total war, absolute weapons, sophisticated irregular warfare – it has become almost impossible to go on saying: 'To fight this war will be less evil than the consequences of *not* fighting it'. The basic reason lies in technology (itself a moral-less system). Nuclear weapons, modern delivery systems and generous supplies of automatic weapons actually dictate what their possessors should do. Instead of serving the policy of their masters, weapons systems determine the character of war.

Today we have an irrational situation in which the superpowers spend their treasure on weapons which logically they dare not use. It is hard to see how you can make a credible threat to do something which would be both immoral and irrational if you did it. Over the past thirty years, official strategists have offered me a variety of chess theories to explain this, but they have never been able to promise me that the Russians were following the same theories. Unless they are, deterrence cannot be stable.

Indeed there is no stability to hand, because there is no

agreed morality, no common view of the nature of humankind. At best there seems to be a melancholy acceptance that there is nothing to be done about the wickedness of man, so we had better be ready to drop the bomb and pray for forgiveness afterwards. For myself, I cannot see how we can drop it, or keep it, or make it and expect to be forgiven. And it is little better – in terms of damage already done, it is actually worse – for the great powers to supply conventional weapons to smaller powers which are all too eager to use them. Britain equips the Argentine Navy, and supplies the Shah with tanks which are used by the Ayatollah. Both China and the United States arm Pakistan, while the Soviet Union, Britain and France equip India. Any diplomatic logic there may have been is corroded by the inscrutability of history, and by the impersonal logic of the arms themselves. Everyone deplores the consequences, yet none of the governments involved in producing these weapons is prepared to withdraw from the market.

This is the point where I have to grant primacy to my conscience over that of my community. I do not impugn my country's motives in arming itself and others: its current leaders do not feel they can honorably do anything else, I suppose. They can lock me up, if they choose, but I simply cannot join in the war game.

In the end I am a peace 'wet', a peace 'nut', because I think somebody has to be. Somebody has to bear witness on behalf of peace if the brakes are to be kept on the chariot of war. Pacifism is something like a catholic priest's vocation to celibacy: you have no right to expect it of others, but you have to embrace it yourself. It is a banner you have to carry as reasonably as you can.

As to whether it is arrogant to claim that I know better than my country (actually my government, which has to believe it is the same thing): the trouble is, I have come to the conclusion there is a higher authority still – namely God – whose interests do not necessarily coincide with what my country now conceives its interests to be. That authority says to me, through heart and mind, no fighting; and, in a way, that is so *unnatural* – so contrary to the instincts of the human animal – that I am all the more inclined to accept that command as coming from God.

I have to remind myself, though, that generations of British soldiers have knelt with their chaplains, quite sure that God was on their side. Which is not much of an argument, since warriors were kneeling with equal conviction under the banners of their enemies. The chances are that God is on everyone's side, hoping they will not kill one another: for He knows what it is to suffer and die.

The Gospels are elusive about the morality of war. Jesus was not interested in fighting Himself, even in joining the freedom fighters against Rome; but He seemed to take war for granted and He accepted soldiers for what they were. The Old Testament shows Jehovah authorising every kind of frightfulness, and the Book of Revelation is a positive festival of warfare. Many good Christians still expect the world to end with Armageddon and even welcome the prospect. Such people tend to believe in an active power of Evil, and argue that against such an enemy the Christian must be ready to fight and die. Indeed, the Christian might care less than the humanist about sacrificing himself, because the Christian believes in a higher form of life to come. None of us, he might say, has any sacred right to live.

I, however, am quite sure that I have no right to take the life of another, and I do not think anyone else has. Judging other people's wickedness is not something I care for, and judging an entire foreign nation is far beyond me. How far back should I go? What circumstances should I take into account? Who provoked whom?

In the end, it comes down to what sort of person you think you are, and for all my pacifism I remain the sort of person who does not trust simple solutions for complex questions. I think we can only make progress by worrying at these problems from every side, and by trying to get as many different motives as possible pulling in the same direction – by trying to unify the pull of head and heart and guts, of reason, faith and instinct. For I am inclined to think that if you can unify them, you are heading towards the will of God.

I should like to think that the peace-maker and the war-maker – the pacifist and the soldier – could pull in the same direction, too, so that they were both moving the world in the direction of being a safer place. No child of ours wants to make war, unless we teach it.

If we cannot just declare total peace, let us at least move away from the delusion of a war that can produce total victory. We must step things down, get away from absolute weapons and total war. In a rather dreary word, we must negotiate limitations. And we must, for a change, talk and act endlessly and urgently as if we meant it. When Mrs Thatcher's speechwriters coarsely accuse the CND of 'hijacking the word peace' they are acknowledging their own failure to give it the meaning and currency it deserves. It will not do for this generation to be told that we could have had peace in 1939 if we had prepared better for war, and that we should do it properly this time. Why should we think the other side will not respond with even better preparations, and the whole spiral move upwards? In any case, for the three reasons we have discussed, this is nothing like 1939.

If we must have weapons for the foreseeable future, can we at least not freeze their designs and limit their numbers by an international system of licensing and inspection, and can we not covenant to return to certain *rules* of warfare? The Geneva Conventions seek to extend protection to prisoners, the wounded and civilians, but they still await the foundations of an actual code of warfare. It is not enough to say the Russians would never agree to any of this: what the

Russians have yet to be confronted with is the demand not just of their ideological opponents but of the whole of the rest of the world that they should do so. To this end we must return to that discredited body the United Nations, and we must restore its credit even if that means surrendering to it some of our precious sovereign powers and permitting it to have – as it was always designed to have – its own substantial military force. I say that as one who would sooner see no armies anywhere upon earth, but can see little alternative to mutual destruction. This really is one world, and it will only take one war to end it.

CHAPTER THREE

The Violent Society

The mounted policeman outside Chelsea football ground looked down with distaste on the youngsters shoving their way in. 'Their dads seem to have given up on the discipline', he said; 'When I was that age my father took his belt to me regularly. Didn't do me any harm.'

I wondered if it had done any good to either of them; but that was hardly the place to argue. The sense of futility, of young energy running to waste, hung heavy over the entire assignment of our film about crime and punishment. If anything, it was even worse during our three days in Winchester Prison: bright, clean, humane, and bustling with all the pointless efficiency of an ant-heap.

At first sight, war, sport and crime seem to have a good deal in common. All three have elements of excitement and fear; all three involve physical violence; all three attract the energies of young males. Attending a Saturday football game, a man from Mars would conclude that human youths positively enjoyed hating one another; for the high-spot of their week apparently consists of a festival of hatred, a thinly disguised mock battle between rival gangs trying to inflict as much damage upon one another as the older generation will let them get away with.

Perhaps it is a pity there is not more playing of sport and less watching of it; for if sport is a way of letting off steam, there still seems to be plenty left after the game is over. Those who watch belong to precisely that age-group which gets into trouble most – young men between the ages of fifteen and twenty-five. Violence seems to be the connecting link, and I fear the male monopoly on it is breaking.

We all know – or think we know from what we read in the papers – that violence is our biggest criminal problem; that murder is on the increase because capital punishment has been abolished, that rape and mugging are widespread, and that if your house has not been burgled this year it will be next, and that more and more criminals are using guns. Most of which is hysterical half-truth. All crime is bad by definition; but Britain's crime record is not *that* bad. Before we embark on this particular moral inquest, it is as well to be sure that the problem is what we think it is.

Statistics were never easier to come by than they are today, and never more dangerous. Much depends on the sources and categories used, and whether like is really compared with like. Far more crimes are committed than are ever reported to the police[1], but fewer still were reported in previous generations. You have only to read the manorial records of mediaeval England, or the report of the Constabulary Commission of 1831, to get a picture of rural violence which makes our twentieth century inner cities look peaceful. Law enforcement was often pusillanimous and (as the Commission reported) juries reluctant to find guilty offenders with whom they sympathised. Contemplating today's England, with its densely packed population and its boundless opportunities for conflict and theft, the amazing thing is that we are so orderly and respectful of one another's rights and property. Our ancestors would have taken it for granted that with so many large gatherings of the working class and so little work for them to do, riots would be inevitable. To them, labour was as necessary for law and order as it was for prosperity. The fact that there is no proportionate connection between crime and unem-

---

[1] Much of the subsequent information is drawn from Home Office Research Study No. 76 by Mike Hough & Pat Mayhew, HMSO 1983

ployment suggests to me that the ordinary citizen is a great deal more moral than he has been given credit for.

As it is, while violence against the person is double what it was twenty years ago, it still only accounts for four per cent of recorded crime. Reported rape is on the increase, too, and every case is appalling: but there are little more than one hundred cases a month in a population of some fifty millions, while murders are many fewer than that. The commonest single crime in Britain appears to be stealing bottles of milk from doorsteps.

For many years past, eighty per cent of all serious crime in Britain has consisted of burglary, theft or the handling of stolen goods. Criminally, we are not a nation of violent thugs, but of greedy petty thieves who want something somebody else has got. There is rather more forgery and fraud reported than there is violence, and we would do far more to reduce crime by locking up our houses and cars securely than we would by sending football hooligans to jail. Shops would do more to reduce the theft of stock by controlling their staff properly than by prosecuting shop-lifters. The greatest single threat to the Queen's Peace is undoubtedly alcohol. If we could bring that under control, we might congratulate ourselves on reducing violent crime by half.

We might do almost as much good, in terms of directing our police and political efforts to where they can be effective, by avoiding sensationalism and cooling down the fear and vindictiveness that sweep through the media from time to time. The British Crime Survey (based on the experience of victims, rather than on police case records) offers many examples of how reality contrasts with stereotypes. For instance, the elderly are the least likely to be victims of crime – the most likely are young men who go out drinking at night. The average household can expect to be burgled only once in forty years, or once every thirteen in the inner cities; the fouling or vandalising of premises is very rare.

The victims of crime are actually less vindictive than supposed: far from insisting on heavier punishments, their demands are closely in line with actual sentences.

The British Crime Survey claims to reveal not a massive crime wave, but the centuries-old phenomenon of unreported crime. It may well be that people are becoming less tolerant of this and are reporting it more – thus sending up the recorded figures. But crimes go unreported mostly because people think, quite sensibly, that there is no point in wasting the time of the police with them. They are the sort of incidents which are better prevented by the public than prosecuted by the authorities. If there is one area where the police really do need to re-think their approach, the Home Office Research Study believes it to be the handling of aggressive young men in general. (It occurs to me that, with the population as a whole getting older and with fewer people coming into the young-aggressive age group, some decline in violence must follow automatically.)

Only a small proportion of the laws of Britain are actually concerned with crime at all; but a large part of this turns upon the defence of private property. It is a crudely Marxist doctrine – actually it is Proudhon – that all property is theft: the idea being that it ought to belong to the community which made it and gave it value. In a country like Britain the community does steal some of it back through various taxes, and it is possible to argue that the scale of taxation is responsible for much of the evasion, cheating and corporate fraud and corruption that goes on.

However, the communism of the ant does not come naturally to human beings. The Bible, for all its sense of the community of Israel, is a firm defender of private property, and even socialist governments, in the West, have not seriously challenged the individual's right to his home, car, television set and a great deal more beside. The assumption is that people would not work so hard if they could not keep a reasonable proportion of what they earn. To be fair, they seek it as much for their families as they do for themselves, and the most durable (if not always just) civilisations have always been based on the handing down of property by those who can acquire it. At the same time, the feeling has grown that quite apart from social justice, the system works better if ownership is scattered and not concentrated in the hands of either a privileged few or of a bureaucratic state. How to achieve the scattering is another matter; but the laws are at least devoted to seeing that any redistribution is done in an orderly manner and not by smash and grab.

A later chapter is devoted to the subject of political morality. For the time being I must observe that British politics have become a constant tug of war between the competing claims of liberty and justice: between the claim that everyone should be as free as possible to make their own choices, and the egalitarian claim of fair shares for all. Both claims have to face the practical query 'But does it work? Does it in fact secure enough to own or to share? Can you run a society based on freedom or on justice, seeing what human nature is?' In fact nobody has ever applied either claim strictly. For one reason or another people's freedom has to be limited, while their share of the cake (even in socialist countries) ranges from a few crumbs to a hefty wedge.

What is a fair share? Should you draw out in proportion to what you put in? In which case, who decides the relative value of the man who designs the car and the one who beats it out of metal? If you give them both the same, on the grounds that both have similar bodies and needs to support, will that actually produce cars?

The point of this excursion into property is to demonstrate that it is an area quite fundamental to the question of crime and punishment, rich in provocation to envy, covetousness and violence; in short, to disorder. Those who rule over us, more or less with our consent, execute laws to avert the chaos which we all dread. Sooner a tolerable degree of unfairness than all Hell let loose.

But laws involve compulsion. If necessary, people are forced to obey them, whether or not they think they are right. Legal justice is not necessarily the same as moral justice; and though it is asking for trouble to let the two varieties drift too far apart it is dangerous to stretch the meaning of the word by alleging that society is actually *violent* in obliging people to obey unfair laws. For me, it is very important that the term 'violence' be restricted to mean *physical* violence. Once society is accepted as being violent, then surely I am justified in hitting back at it physically, destroying life. That is the reasoning of the terrorist, and I cannot allow him to succeed by claiming that only he can offer the oppressed the hope to struggle for freedom. In Britain that has not been true for centuries, and we must see to it that it never is.

It certainly cannot be used to justify the petty thieving which, as we have seen, makes up most of Britain's crime. I am not sure that God is particularly interested in private property (He probably wishes we were less obsessed with it), but He seems to disapprove of the spirit that seeks to acquire it unlawfully. Most children are brought up not to help themselves to property and, once again, orderly life would become difficult if that were not the rule. So why do some people break it? Clearly they cannot all be the victims of unemployment, poor environment or psychological problems, seeing that most of the people who share those disadvantages refrain from stealing and some people with every advantage steal nevertheless.

It has to be faced that stealing is a matter of choice, of choosing either to assert one's will against temptation, or to give in to it. The professional thief has deliberately chosen not to behave as the sort of person who resists temptation, and that may well be the normal identity in his circle. If he gets caught and punished, there is not much loss of face. You do not, however, steal off your mates; for to indulge in most types of deliberate crime it is necessary to deny the brotherhood of your victim (which Christians would trace to the common Fatherhood of God). It is necessary for the victim to be seen as alien to the criminal, or at least as a less real human being – a Pakki, a queer, a stinking rich snob, an old hag. The criminal has to become an egoist, hardened against imagining his victim's suffering, feeling he owes his victim nothing.

Doing what is obviously wrong involves switching off part of one's natural sensibility: not recognising that conscience has any place in the situation. By not exercising one's sense of right and wrong, by not choosing to contemplate the moral choice, it is possible for the conscience to dry up.

The average convict does not complain much about the unjust structures of capitalist society or the temptations of a materialist age. Many criminals find their surroundings meaningless and unworthy of respect. But although society neglects these factors at its peril, they do not justify crime and the criminal knows it.

Nor can we fairly blame the prisons themselves as 'universities of crime'. By the time the average prisoner serves his first sentence he is already well instructed. He takes his sentence as a reasonable response to what he has done: Life is a bit of a game, you win some, you lose some, and if it's a fair cop you take your medicine. Most prisoners have a sardonic sense of what is fair (though they cannot stand sexual offenders or cruelty to children) and there is a sense of order, if not exactly moral order, among thieves. With the exception of a few small Christian missions, not much effort is made in prison to instil one.

The police do not see themselves as moralists at all. As far as they are concerned, a good society is simply one that does not break the law. Christian morality, with its emphasis on right motives and forgiveness, is rather suspect among policemen. It suggests too much do-gooding and not enough discipline. And the police are even more suspicious of attempts to supervise them politically.

Because of this, and because of their operational need for aloofness and security, policemen tend to become isolated and blinkered, their contacts limited to other policemen and to law-breakers, their view of the public jaundiced, and their highest value that of loyalty to one another. Sometimes impatient of the mechanisms of the law they are tempted to get results by cutting corners, even by making deals with criminals, whose background they must sometimes inevitably share. The public cannot expect its policemen to be parsons on the beat or to bring up our children for us. But morally and socially, we have made them a race apart. Too many respectable middle-class families would never dream of putting a son or daughter into the police; though the legal profession (which sometimes defends criminals) is another matter. It can never be good for any occupation to become isolated like this, or it becomes self-preserving with its own private values.

The Prison Service shares most of these tendencies, though in my experience many officers join it with high ideals about reforming and reclaiming the prisoners in their care. That these ideals commonly fade away is largely to be blamed on the impossible task we give them to do and the inadequate time, space and money they have to do it with. The average jail is a powerhouse of youthful energy with no useful outlet, and the moment any constructive work is found trade union pressure is brought to bear from the outside either to stop it or confine it to the most stultifying activity. Added to which, between a quarter and a third of the inmates are less deliberate criminals than addicts, inadequates or mental cases of some kind, to whom a penal institution has no lasting treatment to offer.

But the British are grimly attached to the idea of prison. We like to imagine massive walls with the good people outside and the bad ones locked within, where we hope it is rather unpleasant for them. We are not notably more lawless than anyone else in Europe, yet we persist in locking up our offenders at a higher rate than the rest and at an astronomical cost.

For the British are devoted to the puritan belief that wrongdoing must bring retribution. Punishment, we argue, is not the same as vengeance and need not even yield reform. A morally concerned society must express its outrage, the moral order must be redressed. Some Christians will insist that to ignore a man's personal responsibility – to handle him simply as a case for treatment – is to belittle his human dignity. Now that hanging, flogging and cropping ears are out of fashion, the most serious thing you can do to bring a man to his senses is to deprive him of his liberty. And so we lock him up.

Not even the soppiest of do-gooders proposes tolerating crime. Society, or the moral order, has every right and need to demonstrate its disapproval. But there is more that needs doing than that, or we are merely going through a quasi-religious ritual and one that has little to do with our own religion. For a start, our penal system offers little satisfaction to the victims of crime. Hebrew law was most insistent upon compensation, but ours is surprisingly weak. The law almost brushes the individual victim aside and there is seldom anything to make the criminal aware that he has not just been caught breaking a rule but has actually injured a fellow human being. If the Christian ethic means anything and if authority has any care for the consequence of its gestures, then our penal system must aim to awaken the conscience and produce genuine guilt and repentance, not just a sense of 'You win some – you lose some.'

Rule One of our prison system is that prisoners shall be encouraged (it used to add 'and be fitted') to lead a good and useful life: that they shall be reformed as well as punished. Some prison governors assure me that reform is more frequent than we realise; but clearly, not frequent enough. There are undoubtedly some criminals who must be locked up for long periods, for the public safety. But apart from them, I find it hard to believe that any man is the better for being deprived of his liberty for more than a very short time; and if *he* is no better, neither is the society of which he is part.

Prison is the easy answer. It helps the virtuous to show how different they are from the wicked: 'We are out – they are in.' We hand our offenders over to a kind of penal undertaker to dispose of, buried and forgotten. Almost any other approach would be more difficult, but almost any other would be better. It is particularly unfair upon those we hire to carry it out.

We are not even sincere about wanting to instil that 'good and useful' life. If we are going to send criminals away it seems to me (as it does to so down-to-earth a character as the Duke of Edinburgh, as well) that there should be a clear distinction, with separate staffs and institutions, between that part of a sentence which is meant to punish and that which is meant to reform. The former may well be the work of the old-fashioned prison officer, and the latter that of the chaplain, the psychiatrist and the local community – which for so long has demanded the rehabilitation of offenders, but does very little to make it possible. At least, having made the distinction, we would have to take seriously the business of reformation and stop confusing it with sterile punishment. Even if we persist in locking so many people up we might reconsider this neglected aspect: imprisonment was always supposed to give the criminal time to contemplate the error of his ways and to repent, yet it seems highly unlikely that under modern conditions much of that takes place. With the exception of one or two small Christian missions, chaplains get little support for serious moral exercise or instruction. The attitude of our prison system is not merely secular, but amoral.

Crime is one thing – terrorism, our most topical and headline-seizing violation of the law, quite another. Or is it? By claiming the special category of political crime what the terrorist is trying to do is to place himself under the canopy of warfare, which is no crime. It is not generally held to be wrong to kill and destroy in war, as a last resort, a lesser evil, in a just cause. So every terrorist wills himself a soldier, imagining all the nobility, discipline and toughness that implies. He sees himself as a professional, not an amateur wrongdoer. And, indeed, nowadays he has to be fairly intelligent to keep ahead of the specialised security forces. As we have seen, the very fact that those forces are bound to outnumber him compels the terrorist to adopt what would normally be regarded as immoral tactics like blowing up innocent bystanders. But this, says the terrorist, helps to undermine the oppressors and force the public to take his case seriously.

One grave weakness of all this is that in a mature democratic state, it does not work. Bader-Meinhoff, the Red Brigades, the IRA have not won and cannot win. The societies they attack accept their casualties as part of the price of freedom, hit back and carry on. They make reforms to meet some of the weaknesses picked on by the terrorist, but they do not yield power to him. His very resort to indiscriminate terror reveals that he cannot achieve specific ends: so why does he continue?

The central reason is that, far more than the ordinary criminal, the terrorist has become morally corrupt. His capacity to reason morally, feel morally, react morally has been eaten away and replaced by an image of the sort of person he is, created by man, not God. The hardened terrorist has accepted a baptism of blood as a professional killer which is so monstrous that it is almost impossible to renounce. One needs very few people like this (and perhaps there are only thirty of them in the Provisional IRA) to terrorise an entire province. It is most terrible when, as in parts of Ireland, there is a family pride in it. One of the most appalling things about the 'bandit country' of South Armagh is that it has been bandit country for centuries.

This is not to say the terrorist has no reasonable cause for protest at all. There is usually *some* injustice in the background, though it is commonly less malicious and calculated than the terrorist claims. Because he must *will* to defy his reason and his conscience, he must exaggerate any excuse he can find for doing so. In the end, his movement must devise a new and perverted way of thinking and talking, a revolutionary language which transforms a protest into 'the people's struggle for liberation' and an ordinary, if sorely provoked, police force into 'fascist oppressors'.

Another function of the revolutionary language is to increase alienation; to make the gap between the terrorist and his opponent as wide as possible. By using the revolutionary language the terrorist strengthens his identity and sets his enemy apart as an inferior species, a kind of animal to be disposed of without qualms.

This kind of analysis may help us to understand the mind of the terrorist (a subject on which too little work has been done), but it is unlikely to convert him. He has deliberately put himself beyond the reach of conventional reasoning. What the rest of society can do is to remedy the excuses for terrorism (insofar as it conscientiously can), apply counter-espionage, and resist. At the risk of sounding prim I have to say that I cannot, as a pacifist, employ the terrorist's own violence; but I do not think he has any right to complain if he challenges the state and gets clobbered by it in return.

The more painful side of resistance is that we have to suffer and endure, as the righteous have always done: though we must be careful not to think ourselves so righteous that we could not possibly have given any cause for what is happening. What the IRA does is foully and damnably wrong, but the British have been wronging Ireland for centuries – in the best strategic interests of our own country. It may now seem unjust that we are having to carry the can for our ancestors; at least let us avoid stacking up cans for our descendants to carry.

It will be obvious by now that, for me, violence is the supreme evil, to be placed in a different league from any other crime. I find it unreasonable, immoral, and (like most comfortable, middle-aged and middle-class people) I am terribly afraid of getting hurt by it. Deeper down I fear its power to make me lose control of myself and violate my own moral convictions. Theologically, I would say that violence was an outrage against God's peace and order – that it was the blasphemous destroying of creation. I realise that I am in no position to forbid counter-violence to those who conscientiously feel that force must be met with force: but I am perfectly sure that I am called not to use it myself, and that applies to the punishment of crime just as it does to opposing armed aggression. And because of this vocation it is all the more incumbent upon me to promote alternative ways of crime prevention and peace-making.

It seems to me that violence, and much crime, is really more of an inarticulate language than a deliberate method of getting things done. It is a language of expletives to which we resort when words fail us. The best way of averting violence is to see that words do not break down. It is not just a matter of jaw being better than war, for we have to be careful that the jawing itself is honest and true, that words are used accurately and lovingly and are not poisoned and perverted. For when they are undermined, communication collapses, the language has failed us and there is nothing to do but hit out. And to those who argue that my way of resisting evil has no guarantee of success, I can only reply 'No more has yours – the way of force.'

The nonviolent approach demands a profound respect for language and its meaning. It calls for the greatest care on the part of the media as carriers of our messages from one to another, and for far more attention in our schools to how people express themselves, so that they can communicate without frustration.

It also calls for a readiness to listen, even to things we

would rather not hear; for enormous patience and for the wit to detect half-truths, warped thinking and downright lies. It calls, further, for an openness and a readiness to respond, especially on the part of those who have power; for it is no good teaching people to say what they mean if nobody hears and answers them. Because there is so much noise in the world, because so many of the systems around us are deaf and unresponsive, I have a depressing feeling that many of my fellow human beings have lost faith in words, no longer believe in the possibility of communication, and would rather put their faith in action. To *do* something – almost anything – appeals to them more and more, and usually it means doing something to somebody else.

These gloomy presentiments, though, do not mean I subscribe to the doctrine of Total Depravity I do not think mankind is a load of rotten rubbish, or even that it is violent by nature. It seems to me that man is *ambitious* by nature, eager to establish his identity as a free agent called (by God) to keep reaching forward; but that he constantly mishears or ignores that call, and constantly frustrates and confuses himself by constructing a world that is almost beyond his control. That our crime and violence are not very much worse seems to me a source of some hope.

CHAPTER FOUR

God and Mammon

Even if I live to be a hundred I am afraid I shall never make a convincing Old Boy in the public school sense. I have only been back to my own school a couple of times in almost forty years, and both were embarrassing. The school, in my day, was geared to the winning of scholarships by the anxious middle class. But nowadays nobody seems to need a scholarship and the air is one of relaxed affluence all round. I asked the sixth-former next to me at the headmaster's table what he intended to do when he left? 'Chartered accountancy,' he said confidently, 'and I want to specialise in tax avoidance.'

O times, O morals! And yet I can hardly blame him. It is all very well to say 'Ye cannot serve God and Mammon – consider the lilies of the field . . .' if you are an itinerant preacher in first-century Palestine. But, with respect, most of us have no choice: we have to serve both if we can, but our families, our creditors and our employers are visibly first in line. Mind you, I do not think Jesus was saying that everybody should turn hippy or enter a monastery. His immediate disciples, perhaps. But He must have known that the average man had a living to earn, and He did not regard merchants, landowners or tax collectors as complete untouchables.

Nevertheless, like most of the great religious leaders of the past, Jesus left the impression that making and spending money was not what counted on the road to Heaven, and to this day many of His admirers are confused about the whole business of business. God appears to be saying one thing and Mammon another. Can the two coexist?

As we were reconnoitring the City of London for our film about the morality of business I picked up, in a secondhand bookshop, a different sort of bible on which I was brought up years ago at Oxford. Alfred Marshall's *Principles of Economics*, 1890, is written in the confident ruling-class prose of a man who is not accustomed to being interrupted, and it opens in the following terms:

> Man's character has been moulded by his every-day work, and by the material resources which he thereby procures, more than by any other influence unless it be that of his religious ideals; and the two great forming agencies of the world's history have been the religious and the economic . . . Religious motives are more intense than economic; but their direct action seldom extends over so large a part of life. For the business by which a person earns his livelihood generally fills his thoughts during by far the greater part of those hours in which his mind is at its best . . . The conditions which surround extreme poverty tend to deaden the higher facilities . . . Religion often fails to reach those who have been called the Residuum of our large towns.

The implication is that God and Mammon pull in different directions, and that Mammon wins in the end. Marshall does grant that the Christian Church did something, in the Middle Ages, to stand up for the poor; but it was not until the Protestant Reformation came along, with its emphasis on individual responsibility and initiative, that the liberation of man began; and it was Mammon, not God, that broke his chains.

Had this material progress been bought at the cost of moral decline? Not a bit of it, says Marshall:

> There are strong reasons for doubting whether the
> moral character of business in the modern age com-
> pares as unfavourably as is sometimes supposed with
> that of earlier times . . .

Marshall admits this is surprising in view of the much wider
opportunities for knavery that exist today, and the remoter
relationship between the producer of goods and his cus-
tomer. But Marshall puts it all down to the splendours of
Free Enterprise; though today he would be obliged to
acknowledge a good deal of public supervision as well.

The City of London is a delicate combination of the two:
it is publicly supervised private enterprise. If not the richest,
it is still the subtlest marketplace in the world and far too
intricate to fit any caricature model of itself as a conspiracy
of a dozen dastardly bankers manipulating the nation. The
idea of a market is to make supply fit demand by using
prices to encourage or discourage both – to convey information about what is needed, or that is the theory. But in
some corners of this marketplace it is not just *today's*
demand and supply that people are concerned with, but
tomorrow's, next month's, next year's. That basic human
hankering for predictability and order asserts itself: how to
even out the bumps in the system? That basic human hankering for advantage, too: how to end the game a winner,
not a loser?

And so, in the marketplace of the City, you can buy a
share in a factory you have never seen from a man who has
never seen it either, and sell it (at a profit) to a third man
who never intends to go there, without any of you lifting a
finger on the factory's behalf. You can buy compensation
for accidents that may never happen. You can buy the right
to enjoy crops that have not yet been harvested with money
you have not got. Indeed, you can buy money itself. For the
City brings together those who have money to spare and
those who want money to use, including the government

itself which not only wants money and keeps it here, but prints it, too, and then has to sell it to us. Nor is the game limited to Britain: it involves other countries as well, which takes us into the intricacies of foreign exchange. Do not imagine, either, that this is all rich men's money and therefore has nothing to do with their pocket: if you belong to a pension scheme, a building society, a trade union or a church – if you maintain a bank account or an insurance policy – then your money is among the pebbles on the City beach. If the City is engaged in dirty business, then your hands are dirty too.

But London would never have achieved and retained its eminence if it had not acquired a world-wide reputation for honesty, for keeping its word, paying its debts and not being evasive about either. That reputation was built up, and is still maintained, on the basis of man-to-man honour. My word is my bond, and there is no future for the untrustworthy (or so the City likes to think).

Whatever Marshall may say about the limitations of religion, it is reassuring that so profoundly moral a community should have at its heart St Paul's cathedral and be peppered with churches as lavishly as Rome itself. The money-changers may have been driven out of the Temple, but they still loiter wistfully on the steps and the Church meets them half-way. The Church of England's investments are worth more than a thousand million pounds, and there are other churches and related charities worth almost half as much.

If there is one thing that does not appear on the apostolic agenda it is the accumulation of wealth. And yet, with branches in every parish, stipends and pensions to pay, the Church has more than mere appearances to keep up. Imagine the outcry if it *did* sell all that it had and gave to the poor, and closed down! Yet another network would be established to maintain the buildings, pay the ministry and support the retired clergy.

The Church, then, cannot eschew business. But business does not have to embrace Christianity. Granted there have been sects like the Quakers who have raised the ethical tone at times (though they have no great influence today). Granted also, the puritan ethic of hard work and few holidays (of which much the same might be said). But honesty in business need not have a supernatural basis. The system runs more smoothly if you can trust the people in it, so that it makes good practical sense to keep to the straight and narrow path. Eventually people will stop patronising dishonest traders, so that honesty will be the best policy because honesty pays. Or does it?

The City would like to think so. When somebody lets the side down it – or communities like the Building Societies, the Insurance Industry or the Package Tour Operators – rally round to discipline the delinquent, make good the damage and restore their corporate reputation. The respectable thing in many occupations nowadays is to proclaim a professional code of conduct and police it internally, hoping to stave off the disgrace of government intervention and the law courts.

But, as with the police themselves, this kind of regulation can become an exercise in self-defence: in other words, whitewashing. And when we leave the City and get down to the suburban level of shifty landlords, door-to-door salesmen and fly-by-night double-glaziers, professional honour is not a very potent force. For many injured customers there seems to be only one reliable sanction: an Act of Parliament. The law does not pretend to guarantee virtue, but it does know the rights of property when it sees them; and if you steal from the rich to give to the poor, the law will hand the money right back to the rich again.

I do not want to make excuses for anyone, but I cannot help feeling there are more obstacles in the path of spontaneous virtue today than ever there were in the past. The mediaeval Church might make a great song and dance about the Seven Deadly Sins. But what chance can the average peasant have had to indulge in pride or gluttony, covetousness or sloth? The opportunities were minimal, the propaganda for virtue stern and the penalties for disobedience savage. It was so unlikely that a labouring man would have been able to afford any object of value that mere possession of something valuable was prima facie evidence of theft.

Today, anybody might own a car or a television set. The temptation to covet, envy and lust after things is formidable and inflated by advertising and display. The sheer opportunities that surround us to acquire other people's property dishonestly, to steal, pilfer and cheat, are almost irresistible. Which of us has not quietly nipped round a barrier without paying, taken home stationery from the office, added a fictitious trip to a mileage claim or helped himself to a souvenir from a hotel room? If 'everyone else is doing it', it becomes almost the proper thing to preserve solidarity. That may be the Devil's logic, but again I am surprised that most people are so honest.

A great deal of our moral behaviour towards others is motivated by our affection for them and our capacity to see them as like ourselves. Virtue is made more difficult by the impersonality, the alienation of working life in large organisations. Many of us no longer work for a known individual. We are aware that even the man who gives us our orders, our foreman or department chief, is himself an employee of the organisation. We are not sure who claims our loyalty, for all we know is a logo, a company name, an office building with no human face or feelings, and if we cheat, we cheat only 'it'.

'It' becomes other, becomes alien, and so do those who represent 'It' as management, far away up the ladder. So do those 'It' is meant to be serving, the customers who are really our fellow men and women, who buy the product or rely upon the service. We get so caught up in our struggle to make some impression upon 'It' that they, our public, get forgotten and are regarded as rather a nuisance when they intrude.

One of the things that troubles me fundamentally about this whole question of right and wrong is that I *want* to say, from my essentially Protestant background, that it is all the responsibility of the individual. I find myself resisting the argument that a more powerful factor is the influence of class interests and the structures of society. Nevertheless, the Bible (and especially the Old Testament) does reflect that in the terms of its day. We find the prophets admonishing Israel as a whole, or its priests and rulers, rather than the individual Jew.

I know Christians today who talk about 'sinful structures' or 'institutionalised sin' – terms which I do not care for because I suspect them of being attempts to put the blame on abstract principles rather than responsible people. I want to say 'It is not capitalism that exploits – it is John Smith, who happens to be a capitalist and could easily stop exploiting if he chose to.'

The weakest point in my statement is the word 'easily'; for could John Smith stop, and stay in business? Indeed, how could he stop without withdrawing from business altogether? 'Exploiting' is a poisoned word in any case, and arguments like these are full of words that have become poisoned. Capitalism itself is one, Marxism another, and profits a third. To some people profits equal caviar and champagne, which is a parody of what they are meant to be. Presumably there are some company directors who squander their surplus on extravagant luxuries, just as there are workers who squander their wages on gambling and cigarettes. But if a business does not earn more than it costs to run it cannot pay taxes, buy new equipment, pay dividends to pension funds or employ any workers at all. If it is exploitive for John Smith to sell his toothpicks for more than it costs to make them, then for all of us it is Exploit or Die.

John Smith is as much a victim of the system as you or I. Our freedom of will is real enough, and in the end decisive, but it is invariably limited – by various biases and conditionings and by the systems in which we are caught up. The person of conscience who wishes to maximise free will has to exercise some tricky footwork to avoid being trapped in a position where his or her freedom is, in fact, minimised.

I have been arguing that profits in themselves are not immoral. It is silly to condemn the profit motive as if it were a lust for unlimited caviar. But how those profits are made and what is then done with them can be a different matter, and this is where I begin to see that big impersonal structures may overwhelm the individual.

You have only to watch a big organisation at work or, more convincingly, be employed by one, to realise that it is not and cannot react like a human being. It cannot show love or humour or pity, and it has no conscience to tell it what is right or wrong. It can only have rules and procedures which develop a momentum of their own – a sort of inevitability which can only be deflected with great difficulty and ingenuity. Its very size, which gives the organisation strength in competition, also makes it inflexible. People who manage large organisations often try to present the outside world with an attractive human image of it – the bank that listens, the airline that takes good care of you – but frequently this is an attempt to counteract a reputation for being precisely the opposite. Banks, after all, cannot listen; nor can airlines care for anyone or anything; only individuals can choose to exercise those human functions.

Yet large organisations do acquire characters in the eyes of those who have to deal with them, sometimes alarming or negative ones dictated partly by what they are for and partly by how they affect their employees. The image may be something of a pathetic fallacy, but it becomes a very real influence upon our lives. Banks, for example, are about money. Most of us are worried about money, so we find

banks worrying places. They lock up their employees
behind bars, where we imagine them checking slyly on our
overdrafts, and so banks seem to be 'on the other side'. *They*
do not know how hard we have worked for our money, the
troubles we have been through, how badly we need the
cash: so we suspect them of suspecting us. We suspect all
large organisations of not understanding the human predicament: they are not human themselves, they serve only
their own personal ends. The best way to humanise them is
to break them down into smaller units, or at least intimate
local branches where human relationships can be established once more. But in the terms of the system, this is
often uneconomic.

Behind it all lies money, the root of all – hypocrisy? Most
of us deplore the influence of money, but we are reluctant to
turn it down. In theory, it is a convenient substitute for
barter; but in practice money has developed a life of its own,
breeding, migrating, getting sick, even withering away
from an illness called (paradoxically) inflation. To him who
hath, money is given. From him who hath not is taken
away even the little he had. How can that be part of the
moral order of things?

Bring together the world of money and the world of big
impersonal organisations and there are generated the
poisoned images of capitalism, imperialism, neo-
colonialism and the transnational corporations – all of
which it is fashionable to boo. Yet none of these trends has
been wholly evil; most of them, from a broad view, have
produced a considerable balance of good. And after all,
what purpose is served by booing history? Marx never did,
nor Marshall, and Christians should remember that in the
past they have found no difficulty in justifying everything
from the conquest of Peru to the whaling industry in terms
of the Bible. Can we pass moral judgments on blind economic forces?

We can now, I think; and although it will not bring back

the whales or the Peruvians, it may help to avert future blindness. Because they were building a world for their children on values inherited from their own fathers, the conquistadors and the whalers did not stop to consider morally what they were doing at that moment – the *now* at which the moral choice exists and has its true value. They knew not what they did; but we have far less excuse for ourselves. One factor that makes our moral choices so complex but so urgent today is the weight of information available to us all, to an extent that was not available to our ancestors, and the thoroughness of the analysis based upon it. The conquistadors did not know, or did not wish to know or were incapable of understanding, that the Incas were not primitive savages but a dignified civilisation; and only today are we in a position to appreciate the delicate ecology of the seas. We have been warned, and it will be hard for us to plead ignorance of pollution, deforestation, the destruction of southern cultures for the benefit of northern economies.

I doubt if the average Londoner of the eighteenth or nineteenth centuries had much idea of where the Empire's wealth came from or who had suffered for it. But we have no such excuse when our newspapers and television tell us constantly about the tea-pickers of Sri Lanka, the gold-miners of South Africa, and what happens to the arms we export. We can read all about it in the Brandt Reports, and whether or not our conscience is pricked (for it is, in every sense, not all black and white) we have only ourselves to blame if we drive the Third World into the arms of our enemies. Moral or immoral, it is simply not very clever to allow the Third World to believe that all the benefits of our trade relationships are going to the West.

This is where we have to choose whether to make a choice, or whether to resign ourselves to the system. It is possible that the market system knows best, and that it is futile to fight it. Perhaps supply and demand will balance in the end, the ablest will get the rewards of their imagination and hard work, while the prosperity they create trickles down to the poor. In the long run, goes the argument, it does the Third World no good to live on free handouts or on loans that cripple it with debt (and may ultimately bring down the lenders also) or on artificially high export prices that will drive customers to seek alternatives. It is all very well to grieve for the tea-picker whose life is nasty, brutish and short. But if her wages were doubled overnight the result would be inflation in Sri Lanka, perhaps an even bigger population explosion, and prices undercut by other producers. The last state would be worse than the first. In the world as it is, rather than ought to be, bleeding-heart economics are liable to do more harm than good.

But hard-nosed economics are not as realistic as they pretend, either. Supply and demand seldom achieve stability. The long run turns out to be so long that people drop dead by the wayside. And the prosperity does not 'trickle down'; it gets diverted on the way by those who have power, and already have wealth.

The knowledge of all this undermines the resolution of both sides. The have-nots increasingly know what they are missing, while the haves are uneasy about what they have and how they are getting it. Even though Britain's unemployed are many times better off than a fully employed tea-picker, our unemployment is scarcely a tribute to the system which values people according to what they do and then gives them nothing to do. Nor should we deceive ourselves that Britain has no real poor at all.

So what is to be done about it? There are many conscientious people – not all of them class-warfare Marxists, and many of them Christians – who believe we must dismantle the capitalist market system and install a planned economy for the benefit of society as a whole and the poor in particular. Such people see capitalism as based on individual greed, careless of human brotherhood and the commands of Christ. They argue that Jesus was 'biased for the poor and powerless' and that we should be, too. If the well-to-do and powerful will not surrender their unjust privileges, they must be compelled to do so and deserve no compensation. And if systems and structures have taken people over, then those systems must be compelled to change also. In the course of doing this it may be necessary to disconnect the country from the outside world and permit only such traffic as fits in with the plan.

This may sound like good gospel, but I must confess I am suspicious of it. My pale pink heart would like to believe it, but my head does not, and I think for good theological reasons.

There are not many dangerous heresies but one of the very few is the heresy that if only we can get the *system* right, earth shall be fair and all men wise and good. Men are not rubbish; but they do have an indelible streak of folly and blindness which is drawn to the surface by systems of power. Things are bad enough as they are, but at least the economic system that we have has the merit of being incoherent: it is a mixture of very impure capitalism and very impure socialism. This allows us a great many choices, and choices are to be encouraged because they let in the question of right and wrong. Once a pure and coherent system is installed, it has to be defended without question; and installing and defending it, as we can very well see in Eastern Europe and other would-be socialist states, is a brutally inhuman business. It is not only the rich and powerful who suffer in these so-called revolutions (many of them escape to prepared positions) – time and again it is the ordinary working people who suffer most.

The very claim to be *able* to plan an economy seems to me to be nonsense. Nobody has ever come within miles of it, for it is far too complicated and perpetually blown off course by winds from elsewhere. Furthermore, it is a breath-taking example of human pride; and, pride being what it is, nobody who claims to be planning an economy will ever admit to being mistaken.

Do we then admit defeat, accept that life is unfair and regard the gospels as no more than a promise of justice in the life to come? I think not. I do not see how we can read the Bible, or for that matter any of the great Holy Books, and brush aside their demand that we do something here and now about poverty and injustice. Real faith must lead to good works.

The early Christian ethic of life in the world laid a heavy emphasis on duty and service. Slaves had to obey their masters, masters had to be just to their servants, soldiers had to follow orders, labourers do a fair day's work for their pay. Jesus was, above all, the suffering servant. Revolutionaries have always been critical of Christianity for encouraging a servile mentality and knuckling under to the ruling class, however unjust. 'The Church has always tried to keep people in their place. What about their rights? The Gospel is full of reproaches for the powerful, yet all the Church offers the poor is spiritual aspirin. It offers no practical leadership towards justice.'

For a start, that has never been altogether true; though when the Church has demanded justice it has been as rudely put down by the Left as by the Right. On the other hand, people like Tony Benn acknowledge that *their* kind of socialism owes much more to the Sermon on the Mount, the Lollards, the Levellers and the Nonconformist Conscience than it does to Marx. At the conservative end of the political spectrum, where the Church has survived by becoming an ally of the State, I do believe it has kept the Christian conscience alive in high places and that things would have been very much worse without the alliance. To me, the point is not whether Socialism is more Christian than Capitalism, for I can see religious objections to either. The vital thing is that the Christian conscience should keep gnawing away at both. Both the socialist planner and the capitalist entrepreneur must constantly ask themselves whether their actions are dictated by service to their fellow humans or by the worship of their particular system; whether they are taking a decision because it reflects care for those they are serving, or only a self-defensive pride.

But whom am I serving? Who is my neighbour? This is often at the root of the problem in business ethics: whether one's duty is to oneself and one's family, to one's immediate boss, to one's shareholders, colleagues, workers or country. Often the conflicting demands of several are involved and the problem becomes one of priority or of a balance of priorities. In the end it is decided either by going with the current ('Everybody's pushing up their expenses these days') or by taking hold of an image of oneself as the sort of person who does this rather than that and is content to be so. Most of us prefer to be consistent, and our personal morality is largely inspired by loyalty to ourself. For if we deny ourselves we face the appalling problem of who we are, what to be. I am suggesting that the best thing to be is what God intended and that although this is seldom easy to ascertain, ultimately it will make the best sense of our lives. A Christian would say that it happens to be our duty.

In the gospels we seldom find Jesus thumping the table on behalf of anybody's rights. In his eyes, I suppose, only the Father has rights. Jesus emphasizes service and duty; but *everybody's*, including the master's duty to care for his servants. Their rights are actually the duty he owes them, just as Human Rights are actually the duty that all human beings owe each other. These duties fall particularly heavily upon the powerful, the masters in government or in business, for we are told that the greatest must be the servants of all. Theologically, this follows from being made in the image of God: just as he cares, as a Father, for us, so we have to care for each other. The bigger our family, the greater our duty to care. We are all being called upon to join in the enterprise of Creation, of which business is as surely a part as Adam's toil in the fields.

Seen in this light, it is a kind of idolatry for any system, including a business organisation, to be allowed to serve only itself and to make its employees its ministers. However mixed his motives, the craftsman who dedicated his workshop to the greater glory of God was headed in the right direction, for in using his materials respectfully and serving his customers conscientiously he was acknowledging the divine in both. To give less than one's best, to skimp, adulterate or deceive is to insult the divine and ignore its command that we love one another.

The burden of this can be so daunting that we try to forget it or shuffle it off onto the system. But the system has no morality and is not to be trusted. The individual may have little responsibility for it, but he still has some for himself and he must struggle on to assert what he can. Much of the time he is driven to compromise; but Christianity is not only about what is right, it is about finding the strength to do it and about recovering from failures to do it: I believe both are to be found in cultivating the stillness in which to consult our consciences. If we do that, we will often find that we are not so helpless, the system is not so irresistible, nor will others think us as eccentric as we fear. There really are moments when we can say: 'No. That is wrong. This is my duty.'

CHAPTER FIVE

Right Honourable Friends

I won't drop names here, but I have known too many politicians too well for too long to see them either as supermen or subidiots. A dozen or so of my school and college contemporaries have become MPs, ministers or peers, so I might claim to be well-connected with ruling circles; yet between us there is a great gulf fixed.

For a start, I am a media person, a journalist, and there is the same kind of competitive symbiosis between politicians and journalists that you may see at the zoo between the caged animals and the pigeons who invade the enclosures to steal their food. The animals are obliged to be there, on display to the public, trying to look dignified, while the pigeons come and go as they please, vulgar and irresponsible parasites feathering their nests with whatever they can pick up, much to the resentment of the animals.

But in fact the situation is more devious. Political animals are not always on public display. Sometimes they retreat to their lairs, where the pigeons attempt to spy on them. Nor are the animals quite as resentful as you might imagine. It is lonely being a zoo animal, and the pigeons provide company. The animals also use them to send messages to the outside world, and the pigeons are wise enough to know they are being used. Some of them even develop the ambition to become animals.

But there remains a broader gulf between the politician, who has power, and the ordinary citizen who has not. Its breadth leads to a kind of mocking incomprehension on the part of the citizen, which at least is better than hatred. The British have always treated their politicians like their mothers-in-law: however agreeable as individuals, as a species they are absurd. We put them up, because we cannot do without them, and at once we start knocking them down in case they begin to think they are better than the rest of us.

This is healthy up to a point; but beyond that point lies the danger of total cynicism towards anyone engaged in the business of government: if not active crooks, they must be hypocrites.

I suspect, myself, that there is only one hypocrisy, and that is to accuse others of hypocrisy; for as the poet Louis MacNeice says

> None of our hearts are pure,
>   we always have mixed motives,
> Are self-deceivers . . .

and he adds that the worst deceit is to murmur 'Lord, I am not worthy' and turn your face to the wall. I think too many of us who mock the politicians are in that position, and perhaps it is time we tried to understand the morality of politics, to ask ourselves whether mixed motives inevitably mean hypocrisy, whether power must corrupt, and whether the Church should intervene in politics demanding good Christian policies.

Whether you are a God-believer or not you must accept that human beings are, in some sense, meant to live in communities. We are not solitaries like the rhinoceros or giant panda, and we have got where we are because of our ability to share and collaborate: basically in the family, then in tribes or urban communities and finally in the nation state. 'Politics' come from the Greek word for 'city', the origin of our democratic state, which also accounts for 'policy', the objectives of the state. Clearly, if a number of people are going to live together in anything but wild disorder, there has to be some agreement on the purpose of their common life. There must be rules, so that people respect that purpose and do not merely pursue their personal interests or those of some sub-group. Much of the art of government lies in persuading people that the general plan, or policy, is also in their personal interests. If you cannot persuade them of this, it may be necessary to compel them. Some degree of compulsion is almost inevitable in a complex state; but the more a government has to rely upon it, the greater the risk of that state breaking up.

But how formal do we have to be about our national purposes? Can't we just get on with raising our families and making a living in a civilised manner? Unlike more recent states, the British seem to find no need for a grandiloquent constitution pledging them to life, liberty and the pursuit of happiness, or to liberty, equality and fraternity, and yet we have no less of those blessings than countries which have formally contracted for them (or so we believe). Wisely, we are doubtful of the notion that if things look right on paper they will come right in practice. Some of the worst excesses in history have been committed in fulfilment of elaborate political philosophies.

Deep down, the British know instinctively what their nation is about. It is about preserving a balance between individual freedom and social fairness. Our story for at least three hundred years past has been one of adjusting the scales, now to one side, now to the other, trying to get it right. We never shall, in fact: not only because we are not perfectly wise but also because you cannot, in fact, weigh out freedom or fairness like potatoes. There will always be people protesting that the balance is wrong. Politics is the art of the impossible.

In any case, who decides what the balance should be? We cannot be an Athenian democracy where every adult citizen was entitled to speak and vote, because there are too many of us. So we have to choose delegates or representatives to speak and vote for us. Anyway, not everyone wants to participate in government all the time, for not everyone feels wise or well-informed enough or has the leisure to spare; which is just as well, for (although it is very undemocratic to say so) 'the people' *en masse* are capable of being disastrously wrong about what is good for them, as even the Athenians demonstrated more than once.

Most of us, most of the time, would rather have somebody to do our decision-making for us. We expect the chance to review his performance and throw the rascal out if he has missed the mark, but those who claim there is not enough people's participation in decision-making tend to overestimate the amount of decision-making the people want to do. They must, of course, take the consequences. But who can blame the average citizen for finding today's parliamentary business so lengthy and tedious that he would rather leave it to the full-time professional? It is fair enough to hire a specialist, provided you can also fire him.

But can we trust our representative to represent us? Has he any hope of being able to do so? The British MP is not a delegate under instructions from his constituency, or even its majority. In theory, he is his own man and there is nothing to forbid him getting elected as a Tory, walking smartly across to the Labour benches and sitting there voting against his election pledges for the next five years – nothing except his honour.

More likely is something like this: your MP enters the House of Commons and immediately exchanges a normal, healthy way of life for one of madly unsociable hours, theatrical confrontations and votes dictated to him by his party executive. He votes as he is told to, often without knowing what it is about, and he speaks at the behest of the trade union or business lobby which has sponsored him. He will do such favours for his constituents as he can; but if the word comes down from above to vote for cuts in education, then vote for them he will and no amount of squealing from back home will make any difference. If he speaks at all, it will be to say that his own party is utterly right and the other side viciously wrong. He will only follow his conscience if it does not really matter, and if he is on the government side he will either have or hope to get some minor ministerial appointment. Before long, the real world of half-tones will fade away and he will inhabit one of party political black and white.

That is how it looks to the outsider and with the help of radio and television that is often how it sounds, too. There is surely no more sterile form of communication than a professional interviewer trying to extract an admission of failure from a professional interviewee.

This is something of a caricature – most MPs are not, in fact, such zombies – but if the features are exaggerated, they are all too recognisable. And we all have our share in the blame: we have been persuaded that most of the evils of the day can be cured by getting the system right, by legislation rather than moral conversion, and since politicians are naturally keen to demonstrate a command of events which they rarely possess, it has become a full-time job passing laws that will not work and then altering them when they disappoint. The politicians promise too much because the rest of us expect too much because the politicians promise too much . . . It is not that nothing can be done, but that much less can be done than we would like, and it always takes very much longer.

Legislating is rather like dropping a stone into a very large pond. It takes time for the ripples to reach the bank and they are attenuated by the time they get there. If you impatiently throw in several more stones, they interfere with each other's patterns. No one, it seems to me, understands the cumulative effect of laws upon society and upon each other.

But this is no way to talk, having urged the importance of asserting free will and making choices. Having lived in half-a-dozen countries of varying political systems I still find Britain the most agreeable and humane that I know, and I do not wish to live anywhere else. I think this has less to do with the laws of the land than with the spirit of the people; but if that is political it is deeply instinctive, behind and beyond party. I tried to sum it up, earlier, as a balance between freedom and fairness, liberty and justice.

One might suppose that freedom was the first and basic political instinct – an almost infantile demand to do as one wants. But is that really so? That sort of freedom is selfish and anarchic, it wipes out everyone else's freedom, it has to be limited if it is not to create more frustration than it satisfies. Furthermore this crude freedom is shapeless, unsatisfying, and more than a little frightening to possess. It lacks the order we crave; it is unreliable; it creates nothing. The human child rapidly acquires another instinct for dependence upon authority, and as he grows up this becomes even more important than his instinct for freedom. Throughout his formative years he is made aware that other people – his parents, teachers, bigger children, people in uniform – have power over him, power to overrule his freedom and compel him to do what he would rather not do.

It is easier to come to terms with authority than to resist it. If you give in to it, it pats you on the head and helps to see you fed and sheltered. It will relieve you of many difficult decisions, and if it knows its business you will eventually come to like it, identify with it and look up to it for leadership. There is a natural progression from parents and family to government and party. With maturity, you learn to rationalise your loyalty and convince yourself it is for society's good that authority be obeyed.

There is nothing in the Bible to suggest that authority in itself is evil – or that it must be democratic to be good. Jesus seemed fairly indifferent to Roman rule, though as a Jew He can hardly have welcomed it; and St Paul has a long passage in his Epistle to the Christians of Rome in which he describes government as 'God's agents working for your good', to be obeyed not merely from fear of retribution but out of conscience. The early Christians seem to have been anxious to demonstrate that, whatever their religious difference, they were loyal citizens and no challenge to civil power. They were prepared to render Caesar the things that were Caesar's: the only thing they would not grant him was the worship that belonged only to God.

I said that the Bible did not command democracy, and it would have seemed ridiculous to the ancient world if it had; for government was (and still is) about power, and the people simply did not have power – the capacity to give orders and effect changes. Even today we tacitly acknowledge that there are some people who have a genuine vocation to power, who understand it and how to use it, and they become our political leaders. In the western democracies leadership finds that it can actually achieve more if it has democratic endorsements, which has the additional advantage of effecting the transfer of power without violence when the mandate fades. In theory there is no reason why a self-appointed dictator should not be equally benign, but examples are so rare as to make democracy morally as well as practically preferable.

I think that we, in our democracies, are often uncharitable to our politicians. They seldom seek office just because they enjoy the luxury of being kow-towed to – certainly in Britain the powwowing outweighs the kow-towing – but because they wish to do something with the power that office alone brings with it. What they wish to do may turn out badly, but I have never met an MP who believed he was in politics to do anything but good.

One trouble with Christian moralists is that their highly developed sense of sin tends to make them fearful of the evil potentials of power. 'Power tends to corrupt', said Lord Acton, gloomily, 'and absolute power corrupts absolutely.

Great men are almost always bad men.' Which seems to me a gross exaggeration. There are plenty of powerful men who have done great good and emerged no more wicked than the rest of us. They may not have been saintly; but then saintliness is a full-time job not easily combined with political leadership. I may have cast doubts on the effectiveness of political change, but anyone who does believe in it is likely to behave ruthlessly at times in order to secure the changes he or she believes necessary. But if that is what Acton meant, it is far from corruption.

Under a system even as imperfectly democratic as ours, we have only ourselves to blame if our politicians have lower morals than the rest of us, and I think they would rightly resent any suggestion that they had. One of the functions of a gutter press is to keep an eye on that. The Christian element at Westminster is not negligible and I have found it difficult to meet any Christian or Jewish MP who would confess to any difficulty in reconciling his faith with his career. The average member regards his political work as a service to his fellow men and women, though very few MPs would claim that a divine mandate hovered exclusively over one party rather than another. I know some who regard Socialism or Toryism as essentially wicked philosophies. But when it comes to their Tory or Socialist opposite numbers, they excuse them as products of their upbringing, trapped into justifying what they are stuck with.

It is possible to take the view that there is no distinction between political life and religious life; that the Holy Spirit has a will for everything, if only we will listen for it and that 'Who sweeps a room as for Thy laws Makes that and the action fine . . .' But most politicians would find it impossible to operate that way or to regard every decision as a moral or religious issue: most of them are just housekeeping.

Most Christian politicians would agree that God is

indeed concerned with the secular world, as He is with the spiritual. But they would probably go on to argue that in a flawed world which is unresponsive to God it is not possible to act as one would in a world governed by the Holy Spirit. They might go so far as to say that this is part of the burden that God requires us to bear, and that we are shirking our cross if we pretend to be too pure to contemplate the lesser evil. Love, sacrifice and openness may be the standards when the individual soul is at stake; but the choice is much less clear when the interests of the party, the government and the nation are involved. After all, service to others is a Christian virtue, too, and it may be very conceited to put your own tender conscience before the demands of a community. There may well come a point when the individual feels he *has* to do so. But for a politician who claims to serve and represent others, and not just himself, that point can seldom be reached or the individual should look for some other vocation.

Mixed motives and lesser evils are the very stuff of politics, as they are of most people's daily lives. Most people, however, do not operate in a perpetual climate of radio, television and the newspapers or under constant comment by those who are waiting for them to make a slip. There is something flagrantly unnatural about the political life. The system, with its rules and conventions, takes over and sweeps the politician along in its ritual dance.

The two-sided parliamentary chamber, with its permanent confrontation of government with opposition; the adversary style of debate; the virtual obligation to belong to an organised party, and the need to maintain the morale of those who are out of power by staging exaggerated attacks on government – all of this is inevitable in terms of the game. It is said to keep government on its toes and opposition in training to take over. But it is surely not how reasonable men and women would choose to run a country if they were planning from scratch: nor is the British 'first past the post' system of election, which leaves hundreds of thousands of voters – possibly the majority – virtually ignored. The system is justified as one that ensures *stable* government, as if the British had so dangerous a tendency to instability that they had to be prevented from falling apart by rigging the elections. Equally dubious is the claim that a government elected by 'first past the post' has a national mandate to enact all the small print of its manifesto. It is true that governments are elected to govern; but party executives and party conferences are not, and it is outrageous to maintain that because a bare third of the electorate has produced a majority in the Commons for party X 'The people' have authorized the suppression of fox-hunting, the restoration of capital punishment or the abolition of the House of Lords. Since it is seldom possible to say what major issues a general election has really been about, any devotion to fairness and service rather than ideological domination must concede some form of proportional representation.

Despite the record to the contrary, the British remain half-heartedly dedicated to the pretence that the political act can change our lives without changing ourselves; and there is a desperate straining by the political parties to prove this is so. Conservatives strain just as hard as socialists. Past failures are ignored; news is manipulated; statistics are slanted and juggled, and speeches delivered in heightened political language which is more like advertising copy than reasoned argument: perhaps it has to be, since it reaches the public through media which, in order to be *mass* media, are obliged to oversimplify.

As I shall argue in a later chapter, events are almost always more complex than the mass media have time or money to explain; while Whitehall's notorious obsession with secrecy makes it difficult for reporters to discover what is really going on. Ministers, for their part, are resentful of outside criticism (made all the less credible by the lack of reliable information). They believe that only they know the facts and only they appreciate how good their intentions are and how hard they are trying.

I think the British public, in its folk wisdom, is increasingly coming to realise that the effectiveness of political action is limited. Hence the extraordinary toleration, during the early nineteen-eighties, of high unemployment. Except in time of war, I do not believe the British are prepared to grant politicians any greater powers to take action than they already have. The public has no use for incompetent politicians, but it prefers honesty to cleverness and I think it is less impressed by party uniformity than some leaders imagine. Of all nations, Britain can claim to be politically grown up and can well afford a wider variety of opinion in the media as well as in Parliament, a greater readiness to 'think it possible you may be mistaken'.

Nobody is right all the time: yet that is the impression that party leaders strive to give. Power does not necessarily corrupt, and under the British system nobody has had absolute power since Cromwell (the author, incidentally, of the above quotation). But power does sometimes deceive those who ride on its back. It develops a momentum which convinces the politician that from the top of the next hill he really will see the promised land. The British people know in their hearts that there is no such land, only another landscape which may be better or worse than the last one; and from time to time, when they fear the driver is going to break everyone's neck, they dislodge him or her and hand the reins to somebody else.

Looking back over the past forty years, it does not seem to have made a great deal of difference whether we have had a Tory government or a Labour one. If few of our leaders have been brilliant, none has been actively wicked and the main trends have gone rolling along, like our curious class system which seems to have as much to do with heredity as money. What has been really important in maintaining the humanity of Britain has been the alternation of parties, our devotion to the swing between the party of social fairness and the party of individual freedom. Has there been a moral issue here? Is Socialism, for example, really more just, more Christian, than Tory Capitalism?

The Bible has been claimed as giving divine approval to private property and the creation of wealth, though it must also be granted that it makes us God's trustees for the world, charged with tending it carefully, relieving poverty and not becoming obsessed with riches. That we have failed to do these things – not totally, but deplorably – can hardly be denied. Contemplating our own unemployment, the plight of the Third World and the pollution of the planet, surely there must be a better way of sharing the gifts of creation?

It is true that in Britain and most of the North-west our system has brought us much to be thankful for: that we are free of starvation, plagues and concentration camps. But the positive freedom to create things, to make changes and even publish your views depends a great deal on whether you already have money and power. We may have the essentials of liberty, but what about equality and fraternity? The ancient cry of the English people, 'When Adam delved and Eve span, who was then the gentleman?' still reproaches us. Can it be fair, can it conceivably be the will of God, that so few people should control so much of the wealth upon which depends the welfare of the rest of us?

The obvious starting point for reconstruction is a primitive socialism: the brotherhood and sisterhood of mankind, with fair shares for all and privilege for none. Christians confess that the sinfulness of man tempts him into wrong choices, so why not remove the temptation? We might even concur with Marx that Capitalism is so inherently sinful a structure that those who achieve power in it cannot avoid treating their workers inhumanly; so the structure must go, and be replaced by one that is planned fairly on behalf of the working man, who is the poor and oppressed of the New Testament.

And yet, is he? The poor are with us still, and even those who are only *relatively* poor suffer the same anxiety and contempt as ever. But Marx would have been astonished at the living standards enjoyed by the modern European worker, even when unemployed, and by the extent to which he does, collectively, influence our society. Yet the attempts which have been made to remould society along socialist lines have demonstrated that power is not something that can be averaged out – it remains an individual vocation. Just as capitalist freedom is very limited unless you have the power to enjoy it, socialist equality also becomes a framework for the use of power. It turns out not to be a good in itself, but a different set of opportunities for human beings who are essentially the same as they ever were.

I do not regard Marxism as a political dirty word. It has got some things right but like all theoretical systems it has become addicted to its own logic. It has gone far beyond the science it claims to be, and in the shape of Soviet Communism it has become a pseudo-religion, nothing less than an attempt to explain reality. However, while it has all the dogmas of a religion, the pious jargon, the creeds and heresies, it has the fatal weakness of admitting no mysteries and recognising no God; thus it has no escape from its own fallacies and no appeal from its brutalities. The vital thing about the Christian God is that He is human as well as divine. He understands things like pity, love and suffering and can respond to them through the human conscience. Further, He constantly reveals new things, freeing us to speculate, experiment and make choices.

The pseudo-religion of Soviet Communism, with no external source of revelation, cannot afford such creative luxuries. It can only assert the abstract logic of the system and enforce it ruthlessly; for to lose power is to falsify its own claims and thus annihilate the faith of its own believers. Since it is most unlikely to command the power of capitalist wealth, it can only achieve power by force or subversion. Given the choice of being ruled by the rich or by the violent, most of us can recognise the lesser of the two evils.

Fortunately we in the democracies do not have to make so stark a choice. Our socialists are half-hearted Marxists and our Tories compromise their capitalism. I cannot see the mandate of Heaven in either philosophy, and neither can work perfectly in the hands of imperfect human beings. So it is prudent to average out their faults by seeing that neither holds the stage for too long, and by seeking to ensure that all parties are infiltrated by politicians who are aware of the supremacy of the Christian conscience.

The Christian view of God is a confused and incomplete one, but at least it asserts that, while He knows what we should be and wills our welfare, He has also given us our own free will. I think this means that there is no escape from our duty to care for one another and especially the less fortunate among us, but that there can be no divine textbook setting forth the details of precisely how we should go about that. It is up to us to make things work, but to see that practical efficiency does not itself become a God. As that redoubtable Elizabethan, Richard Hooker, wrote:

> Unless the last good of all, which is desired altogether for itself, be also infinite, we do evil in making it our end . . . because in desiring any thing as our final perfection which is not so, we do amiss.

It seems to me, then, that if politicians are to avoid 'doing amiss' they must seek to serve the will of God and not merely the reputation of their party; and that in gospel terms that will amounts to caring for one another, and especially for the disadvantaged. Whatever St Paul may say about justification by faith, there can be no doubt (from such passages as the separation of the sheep from the goats in Matthew XXV) that good works are expected, too.

Does this mean that the churches should be active in politics? This is a peculiarly Anglican problem, for it has never occurred to the Church of Scotland, the Roman Catholic Church or the Methodists that they should do anything else; nor has it occurred to the government to bother much about them. It is the feeling, indeed the constitutional fact, that the Church of England is part of the ruling Establishment that makes government so resentful when the C. of E. steps out of line. In practice this usually means the Tory line, for the Labour party has never grown used to having an Anglican chaplain nor to expecting Anglican support as of right.

Why the Church of England should be expected to keep out of politics now when it never has done in the past is a fairly shallow mystery: though there is a difference between showing a concern for political issues and accepting one party's whip, which would be counterproductive. It seems to me that at a time when many people are becoming disillusioned with economic and political commentaries upon life, there is positive value in having an alternative independent source of comment from a religious and moral viewpoint. Too many countries which lack such a source have found themselves at the mercy of totalitarian systems, and it is curious that the people who deplore the political commitment of liberationist priests in Latin America often turn to praise the commitment of the Catholic Church in Poland.

This is not to say the Church can be a substitute for a political party or that it should seek to create a party of its own. If its priests are pastorally active, it should be as well informed as any party about the opinions of the people; and if its moral theologians are up to the standards of the best universities, it should be as well equipped as they to pass ethical judgments. But I have some doubt as to whether the British churches do now attract a high enough calibre of thinker, or whether they command the necessary social and economic research with which to challenge the secular powers on their own ground.

What Christians, high and low, must do out of their own experience is to stand up and prophesy against authority whenever it is thoughtless, cruel or dishonest; whenever it puts its own survival before the service of the people. Whatever the individual Christian may feel called to do, the Church as a whole should be rather a bad party member, an unreliable supporter of right or left. Its political function should be to haunt the politician, telling him what he would rather not hear.

CHAPTER SIX

In the Family Way

One of the subtlest jokes in literature is to be found at the end of the Hindu Kama Sutra – that exhaustive catalogue of coital permutations:

'Let it be known that the sage Vatsyayana composed this work after observing the strictest celibacy. It has therefore not been marred by any passionate motives . . .'

Now, far be it from me to tackle the subject of sexual morality with prurient or censorious motives. But I am no Vatsyayana. Deprived of sex, I would be living in a world without sunlight. But I have to admit that my experience is frankly old-fashioned: heterosexual, married to the same wife for more than thirty years with no extracurricular affairs or fancy fetishes and no colourful adventures to relate, I must seem a square and boring guide to the subject. Put me down, if you will, as lucky or unenterprising; but please do not think I am holding myself up as an example of how easy it is to be virtuous. As a journalist travelling the world I have hardly led a sheltered life; my imagination is as lively as yours; and some of my closest friends are either divorced or cohabiting or following sexual patterns of life which I would not want to imitate. (How awkward it is, by the way, that we still have not found a way of introducing such couples: 'This is Moira and her – er – *friend* Richard', or, more awkward still, 'Belinda'.)

Awkwardness of this kind is a sure sign that morality is shuffling its feet in the background. Sex and morals have been shadowing each other like cops and robbers since the

Garden of Eden, which seems oppressive when sex is surely one of the most natural things about the human condition and nobody blames the animals for doing what comes so naturally. Today you do not even have to risk producing a baby if you do not want to.

It is easy enough to reason why people should not lie or steal or kill one another: civilised life becomes impossible if such behaviour is not discouraged. But what harm does a spot of friendly fornication or amiable adultery do? As for that solemn ecclesiastical pantomine about 'Till death do us part . . .' – in practical terms it is clear that it is not and need not be true. Why bother to say it?

I do not, as it happens, hold a rigidly high church view of the indissolubility of marriage; but I do believe that the old style family actually suits human nature best, and that society is making trouble for itself if it allows that framework and the morality derived from it to rust away, leaving nothing in its place. I believe that monogamous fidelity – one man formally and seriously pledged to one woman for life – is the best way of integrating the demands of head and heart and guts, and that it is *right*. I would cite the will of God at this point, but perhaps that is only a short cut through everything that follows.

But why should sex raise so many moral issues? For the average person, moral dilemmas probably arise more often in a sexual context than any other context, and the reasons are very complex. The gut reactions we call our sexual instincts are powerful, deep and primitive. Like all living organisms, we are programmed to perpetuate the species: to get children, though we cannot do it singly. It is intriguing to contemplate what would happen if we did, in fact, perpetuate ourselves on the basis of one-for-one replacement without any coupling: the usual explanation is that by requiring two sexes to come together Nature allows enough variety to develop for the species to adapt to almost anything, but this seems to me to underestimate the moral importance of loving and choosing. Be that as it may, the urge for sex is part of the urge of creation. No sex, no Beethoven, no Shakespeare, no Henry Ford or Blackpool Tower – was it the phallic pride of that tower which drew us to make this part of our series in Blackpool? And Nature – God, if you prefer it – seems to have baited the tender tr ɔ by making sex, for most of us, a very great pleasure indeed. Its foreplay spills over into the way people dress and walk, the way they look at one another in the street, and into their arts and recreations where it sometimes degenerates into a series of winks and nudges. The borderline between the erotic and the offensive is highly subjective, but life would be the poorer without sexual titillation and I, for one, resent efforts to ban it.

But if sex is fundamental to life, it is also a somewhat limited activity. One cannot be at it all the time. Lovemaking by itself cannot put sheets on the bed or bread in the mouths of the consequences, so there is work to be done and perhaps more intellectual things to attend to. Sooner or later we have to get out of bed and go about the business of being a community. Clearly nothing is going to make for more disorder there than an undercurrent of sexual free-for-all, so the community has always had rules of some kind dealing with sex, marriage and the family.

There is no point in denying that for a very long time indeed women and children have been treated as the property of their menfolk, though not always property that it was easy to dispose of. We probably underestimate the extent to which, in past centuries, there was genuine affection between husband and wife; but a marriage between two powerful families often looked more like a contract or treaty than a romance, and the lower one moved down the social order, the less point there was in formality. To find a secure position in life rather than a romantic vocation was the objective.

The feeling of *belonging* to one's partner, of not being

available to anyone else, remains. It is, of course, a voluntary giving of oneself as, in theory at least, it always was; and there are still plenty of wives who do not think it demeaning to be subservient to their husbands, indeed who take a pride in doing it well and sharing the joint achievements. In any case, the unfairness of this is breaking down now that a woman can (other things being equal, such as her education and opportunities for employment) support herself if she wants to. A wife's dependence in the past arose from her constant child-bearing, the male monopoly on bread-winning and the family's anxiety to keep its own to itself. We can afford to frown upon female dependence today because we no longer have to secure for women all the things it secured in the past.

Some people talk today as if sex would never have presented any problems if only the Christian Church had not muddied the water with guilt, as in St Paul's grudging admission that it was better to marry than to burn but best not to touch women at all. Some others talk as if sex only started going to the dogs when the Church lost its grip upon marriage.

It is true enough that for centuries the Church saw relations between the sexes as a terrible distraction from the life of the spirit and a rival to its own discipline. The celibacy of the clergy (optional in the Eastern churches) was enforced in the West partly to concentrate the mind by imitating Christ, but partly to keep church property in church hands by preventing the clergy from leaving it to their sons. So far as the laity were concerned the odd thing is that for so long the Church was in two minds whether it wanted anything to do with common marriage at all. It tended to follow the ancient Roman view that marriage was a contract established by the consent of the two parties, and it did not wholeheartedly declare for a public ceremony before a priest until the Council of Trent in 1563. Taking their lead from St Paul, the fathers of the Church spoke of marriage as at best 'a lawful remedy for concupiscence' and at worst a penalty for original sin. Abelard, whom one might have expected to be more understanding, taught that 'to bring home a wife is not meritorious for salvation, but it is allowed because of incontinence'. Even the Council of Trent declared its anathema on anyone who maintained that it was not better to remain virgin or celibate than to marry.

It is hard not to trace this back to Christ Himself; for despite some Gnostic whisperings it is the firm tradition of the Church that He was celibate, and the gospels record several remarks indicating that He saw marriage as a distraction from the Kingdom. Some of my Jewish friends take this as further proof that He was not a regular Jew, for Jews have always been devoted to family life and one might have thought the Old Testament would have endowed the Church with some enthusiasm for procreation. Far from it: for lurking in the background was the ancient heresy – probably of Manichaean origin, though it has captivated many holy people – that the flesh is to be mortified and despised and only the spirit revered. Without wishing to depreciate their insights, I think it is true to say that religious experiences come more readily to those who practise physical austerity. Even when pitchforked Nature came hastening back, the saints felt themselves obliged to speak of marriage as a spiritual union with Christ and to describe their own vocations as a higher form of matrimony.

To suggest, as almost every church has done, that God's gift of sex was something to be ashamed of seems to me a form of blasphemy. If it is possible to accept bread and wine – basic foodstuffs – as sacramental conveyors of the love of God, why should it be so hard to accord the same dignity to the basic act of human affection? But it was nineteen hundred years before the Church could bring itself to acknowledge, at the Second Vatican Council, that the act could be seen as of value in itself ('tending to dispose the spouses to cooperate generously with the love of the Creator') and not just as a means to the conception of children. I find it very hard to resist the conclusion that birth control had forced the Church to acknowledge that sex could be virtuous, beneficial and holy even when the possibility of children had been deliberately eliminated. Every Christian married couple knows this, and most of them would be justifiably resentful at being told they were no better than casual fornicators.

So the Church has altered – or as catholic theologians would prefer to say 'developed' – its attitude to sex, provided it is married sex. If you can't lick it, organise it. Appropriate it to your own ends. Thus the Service of Holy Matrimony in the Book of Common Prayer:

> Marriage is an honourable estate instituted by God, signifying to us the mystical union that is betwixt Christ and His Church . . . ordained for the procreation of children . . . for a remedy against sin and to avoid fornication . . . and for the mutual society, help and comfort that the one ought to have of the other.

Who seriously believes that John and Mary, who have been lusting after one another for months and were probably in bed together last week and who have no intention of producing children for another four years, have anything sinful or mystical about them? And what a patronising way to speak of them! First the Church tells the couple they are really a symbol of what *it* is doing; then it says that as they are liable to have children they had better make it respectable; and finally it tells them to take care of each other, which is what they had in mind in the first place.

But I deliberately distort the case. If you image that all a couple can really do is to lie together, perhaps get pregnant, and cook one another's breakfasts, then the language of the Prayer Book may well sound pretentious. But the Church (and, come to that, secular psychology) does not take so low a view of human nature; nor do they take an impossibly romantic one. It does not follow, just because you have fallen in love, that you will live happily ever after automatically. Anyone who has sweated out a marriage, successfully or unsuccessfully, comes to realise that there is more to it than institutionalised sex, breeding and housekeeping. We undoubtedly are a type of animal with animal instincts and needs, but we are extremely complicated ones, living in an unstable environment, and we take far longer to reach maturity than our four-footed friends – if, indeed, some of us ever do.

Just as no colour means anything without another in relationship to it, so everything we know about ourselves is bounced off other people, from our mother's breast onwards. We cannot even love and value our own body if she does not love it first, which is what every painting of the Virgin and Child tells us. What it dares not say is that love and resentment go hand in hand, trying to maintain a perilous balance between the needs of self and the need for a loving relationship that confirms oneself.

Next we seek integrity, wholeness. We search for experiences that confirm that we are being what we are meant to be and not just living a lie. Marriage is a direct heir of childhood; and just as the child gets those confirming experiences from his or her parents, so the adult seeks them from a partner of the opposite sex. This relationship can bring an added strength as well: searching for their wholeness, people often find subconsciously in others a part of themselves they have lost touch with. We all know flamboyant husbands married to shy wives, or women who are somewhat mannish mated with womanish men – happily married, as well. It makes a mysterious sense of the two becoming 'one flesh', more complete together than they could ever be apart.

And what of that nonsense about 'signifying the union betwixt Christ and His Church'?

The notion is a poetic one, admittedly, but poetry is not

meaningless simply because it does not correspond with measurable facts. The Church is all who acknowledge the fatherhood of God; it is not confined to the ordained clergy. And whether we gain the experience through Holy Communion, prayer or the Gospel, Christians do experience that God still lives in us as Christ today. Love, say Christians, is God; and when two Christians unite in love, that is what they show to the world: the unity between their will as Christian lovers and the loving will of God.

As for the bits about marrying to have children and avoid fornication, here we embark on some longer arguments.

We should not deceive ourselves that fornication was invented by the rubber goods industry. The countryside has always provided more cover for the experiments of young love than the towns do, and if you examine the country registers of a century ago it becomes pretty clear that for half the population a wedding meant the girl was pregnant. Indeed, in some areas I know, every other baptism was entered 'Father unknown'. The Church wagged its head sadly, christened the child and pinned the parents down to their responsibilities, which was surely no bad thing. Economic conditions change and it would be callous to make the production of bastards a crime, but as a general rule there can be little doubt that children are still happier raised by two parents who remain faithful to one another.

There is also much to be said for proclaiming this with some ceremony. Rites of passage are not to be sneered at; it is better for society to know who belongs to whom; and it does concentrate the mind to stand up in public and declare it with the wider family of friends and relatives pledging their support. It is fashionable for young people to shudder at the mention of their relatives and talk of them as uncalled-for interlopers, but in fact they can prove a great source of strength and understanding, friends before whom one does not have to put on an act. If the couple marrying are Christian believers, the ceremony will also tell them they have the support of God and His Church as well, and some churches – though not enough – offer marriage education beforehand and counsel or renewal of vows after. It makes a civil registry wedding seem rather insubstantial.

And yet I seem to be talking about a Victorian twilight. Divorce goes onwards and upwards, civil marriages are now the majority, and no marriage at all – living in what used to be called sin – has become the convention among my children's generation. Middle-class parents agonise over the 'separate rooms or double bed' problem when their children come home with a friend; and dare one ask whether Cynthia is on the pill?

What one cannot do – especially when the children are so careful of one another and quite the opposite of promiscuous – is to cry: 'Never darken my doorstep again!' In many cases that I know, the Church of centuries past would have said the children *were* married, if not formally blessed; and if these young people (hardly children any more) are not professed Christians they can hardly be required to take vows at the altar. Either their consciences are clear or they are suffering from what the Church would call invincible ignorance: either way, it is hard to convict them of sin. They see that the formality of marriage is no guarantee against divorce, and they are too honest to take holy vows when they do not believe in holiness. Personally, I cannot blame them: I can only blame myself and the Church for failing to show convincingly that there is any connection between a good and lasting relationship and a Christian relationship. I try to comfort myself that the youngsters owe their decency to their Christian background, though it worries me whether that heritage will be passed on without Christian commitment. At the same time, I cannot honestly tell them they are headed for hell fire because I do not believe that they are. If anyone is damned it will not be for getting married improperly, but for behaving wickedly however they were married.

It seems to me that sexual relations are enriched when we ndow them with sacramental significance, adding, as it vere, another dimension to them. But sexual immorality is not just a matter of the absence of the sacramental: it is nhuman, degrading and sometimes dangerous for one person to exploit another sexually as a mere instrument for his own ends. I can excuse the erotic in a way that I cannot excuse the pornographic, because it seems to me that while he erotic can help people to take mutual joy in each other he truly pornographic always implies the violent domination of one by the other, an inequality, a lack of respect.

Even the Church has come to recognise that sex is not just an instrument towards fertilisation or the venting of lust. At its best it is a tender and mystical *communication* in which two people express more deeply than words can say what they are and have been and will be to one another; and that can take years to arrive at, indeed it may never end.

At the risk of being accused of puritan repression (for example, of advertising syphilis or herpes as punishments sent by God) it has to be recorded that the wages of old-fashioned sin can still be a very uncomfortable time indeed. Despite the best efforts of the pharmaceutical companies, promiscuity can damage your health and the pharmaceuticals themselves are a mixed blessing. Venereal diseases keep bouncing back in drug-resistant mutations and Britain has recently experienced its first deaths from a new disease apparently reserved for male homosexuals. As so often, conventionally moral behaviour is also practical commonsense.

What are Christians to say of those who have pledged themselves to lifelong fidelity and then divorced? Jesus seems to have taken an uncompromising stand against remarriage, though the churches have one by one made their excuses and sidled away, and the state now completely ignores Him. The fact is, there is now no way of keeping a couple together if they do not want it: the economic sanctions have gone, the social shame and, to a great extent, the religious penalties too.

It may be that divorce is too easy, but that is hardly surprising when marriage is easier still. We expect people to undergo instruction and examination before they can place others at the mercy of their cars, but there are very few qualifications needed before a couple place their entire future in each other's hands, nor could it be enforced if marital competence were demanded. Many divorcing couples should and could try harder – they need help which is often not available. But there are some marriages which have become so cruel, or were always so ill-founded, that it would be even more cruel not to dissolve them and allow both parties another chance. It makes little difference to the human facts whether the marriage was secular or religious.

But what about the divine, the moral facts? If conscience is meant to be the voice of a loving God, can it demand that we suffer? It certainly can, and there are brave people obeying it every day and refusing to take the easy way out; and Christians would say that we do not suffer for suffering's sake, but for the resurrection that comes out of it. When there is pain in a marriage (it may be infidelity, quarrels, drunkenness, violence) that is not necessarily the cue to dissolve it. It is often a sign that something else is wrong and that it is time for growth or rebirth. For a marriage and the people in it must develop all the time, and if they develop out of step with one another the marriage will cease to make sense for them.

It is curious that the Church, so anxious to prevent divorce, has allowed it almost without question in the case of adultery. It seems to be another example of how the marriage relationship, although dressed up in spiritual language, has been regarded as something basically carnal. I am at one with John V. Taylor, Bishop of Winchester, who got into trouble for saying that adultery was not necessarily unforgivable: I do not believe that Christian morality requires divorce at the first act of betrayal. Forgiveness – *and repentance* – are essential to the Christian way. Perhaps the key to the question is the matter of *seriousness*. The service of Holy Matrimony makes it very clear that sexual commitment is to be the signature on a very solemn covenant, and to cheat on it is to show that you are not the sort of person who takes that covenant seriously and therefore does not take himself or his partner seriously either. When it comes to the point, you are not obliged to shack up with that blonde in order to preserve your identity; but you are obliged to keep your promises if you are to maintain a consistent membership of the moral order, the Kingdom.

Is there then no moral release? The Catholic Church recognises, increasingly, that some marriages are null and void because the partners were simply incapable of understanding or fulfilling what was required, or never intended to: in short, that there was no real marriage in the first place, so that any remarriage would qualify as a first marriage. I have known some ingenious casuistry under this doctrine, but in human terms it produces some very wise results; for Rome has a way of clothing sound modern psychology in what appears to be out-of-date mediaeval doctrine. Would that the Church of England were as subtle!

It seems to me a generally observable fact that men and women stand the best chance of developing mature personalities if they promise to pair off faithfully and not shop around for sex; that their children stand a better chance, too; and that it is more natural and agreeable to live as part of a larger family whose members can back each other up, without stifling each other, over two or three generations. Certainly that is how the Church sees humankind to be designed by God, and that is what it seeks to preserve in Christian marriage.

To some this will seem too high an ideal. Since we are not perfect and since the world we have made to live in is far from perfect, we are bound to fall short of the mark and we are bound to compromise. Yet even the divorced find themselves still drawn to the ideal, and we would surely do better to tackle the world's imperfections than abandon that ideal.

Marriage today is in a pressure-cooker. Many who embark upon it expect too much of it too soon: they expect it to transform their lives instantly, for they expect too much of each other. Now that religion is absent from so many lives, many couples – confronting each other face to face – have nothing but each other to look to for meaning. There are endless choices to be made, and very properly the woman now expects equal rights in making them. From every direction come the demands of the job, the home, the consumer society, the media, the social set and the tax man. People are required to deal with a more bewildering variety of problems than ever confronted their grandparents, and the strain lies heaviest of all upon women.

It is nonsense to pretend that woman is not uniquely qualified to bear and bring up small children – or that she is not as capable as man of doing a good job outside the home. But we do little as a society to help her do both at once, although that is what we expect of her. Society expects her labour, if only to help pay its bills, and it assumes she will also tend the family. But if society is not careful it may find it has lost everything: no jobs for women, no real homes, very few children, and those there are scattered through broken families.

We still take the family for granted, to bring up the new generation, feed and house the generation now at work and care for the one in retirement. All our social services are supplementary to the family and based upon the assumption that the family is doing the basic job. But if we really believe in the family, we have got to stop battering it with worry – worry about both the present and the future. Economic stability and international peace are not just governmental ideals, they are essential conditions for the welfare of the family.

Government, certainly in Britain, has to make far bigger family allowances (more generous still, perhaps, for those who are formally married) so that women can move in and out of employment without disadvantage to the family income. There may be protests from the childless who will have to pay for it; but they were children, too, once, and today's children will have to provide tomorrow's old-age pensions.

And if government really believes the family is of moral value, it has to see it is taken seriously in our schools: not just clinical sex-education, but morality and human relationships, subjects so demanding that we hardly dare to teach them; and yet if they are not taught we all suffer the consequences.

Once it was the Church that taught such things, though often with deep embarrassment, obscure language and threats of damnation. That was not only dishonest – it will not work any more. If church marriage is to survive as the highest calling for those who choose it, then couples must be prepared for it fully and frankly, even at the risk of turning away those who cannot face its demands. If Christian marriage is worth having it must be shown to be worth having, and it cannot be easy.

The Church itself has to face the reasonable demands of loving couples who must live in the world as it is, and those demands now include contraception. The Catholic Church long based its opposition to artificial contraception on the arguments that it was a device of lust, a denial of life, an unnatural barrier to God's Will that men and women should go forth and multiply. All of those arguments *can* be true or, as millions of couples could testify, insultingly untrue. Sex, as we have seen, is not a purely procreative activity and it reduces people to the level of beasts to tell them they may not make love unless they are prepared to breed.

That would be a crude and cynical view of love-making. I think many couples would admit that part of the joy of

love-making lies in its celebration of fertility. But it is surely
more than a mere churning out of human infants for the
sake of the score: the extra that is generated does not have to
be a baby – indeed, even without contraception, most
couplings are not fertile. Whether there is contraception or
not, a human relationship, an insight into the love of God, is
being realised. The Second Vatican Council could appreciate that, even if it did not have the courage to say that the
insight was just as valid when contraception was used as
when it was not.

Whatever Rome has to say, most British Catholics, like
most Protestants and non-believers, use contraception with
a clear conscience. They also resort to abortion, and I have
to say I am much less tranquil about that; for clearly life is
not just prevented or postponed, it is destroyed. As with
divorce, however, I do not think the moralist should leap to
the conclusion that it is always done lightly. We have no
right to assume that such release is bought without long
anguish and lasting doubt. The fact that divorce and abortion are now so easily come by does not mean that, for
conscientious people, they are any less painful to decide on.
Some of the moral areas I have been discussing have been
comfortably academic: relatively few of us are generals or
judges or politicians. But sex, marriage and parenthood
touch almost all of us. We all know they are compromised.
We all know we could have done better. And we should all
have mercy upon one another.

CHAPTER SEVEN

Publish and Be Damned

I once met a diplomat at a cocktail party. 'And what's *your* line?' he demanded, inspecting me like a newly hired foot-man.

'I'm a journalist', I told him.

'Pity,' he said, moving away stiffly, 'You *sound* quite a decent chap.'

I might have redeemed myself, a little, by calling after him 'But I'm with *the BBC . . .*', for there is (or was then) a feeling that the BBC and The Times were marginally more respectable than the rest of the rat pack. You may remember that line in an otherwise forgotten play, where the butler enters the library and announces: 'Three journalists to see you, my Lord – and a *gentleman* from The Times.' There were, in my day, still gentlemen with the BBC; and I dare say there still are, what with Robin Day's knighthood and Robert Fox's medal, but I was brought up in the stately days of radio, whereas television seems to demand a certain brashness.

Also a certain ruthlessness if the job is to be done on time. Alas (though I have never worked with one, of course) there are camera crews crashing through the country leav-ing behind them trails of blown fuses, shattered furniture and ruined maidens; not to mention the distorted inter-views that appear later. But they are mere beginners com-pared with the long and dishonourable tradition of Fleet Street, its cheque-book journalism, doorstep sieges of the bereaved, guerrilla photography and downright fabrications. Branded with such a reputation, how can a moral person – let alone a Christian – embark upon or defend a career in journalism?

And mere vulgarity is not the end of the criticism. Even when journalists put on three-piece suits and move soberly through the corridors of power they arouse deep suspicion in the breasts of those who work there that they are enjoying the prerogative of the harlot throughout history: power without responsibility.

We have already seen how the politician convinces himself that since only he is at the heart of the matter, only he appreciates the complexity of the problem, the rightness of the solution and the worthiness of its motives. His critics are jealous outsiders who refuse to understand what he is about, and the worst outsiders are half-informed journalists who manage to get halfway inside, but merely as voyeurs looking for something entertaining to write. They claim to be serving the public interest, but the public can neither hire nor fire them, and if journalists bring down the government they suffer nothing. It appears that a profession which has nothing to win or lose from the consequences is able to alter the way people think and so persuade them to act in ways that would never otherwise have occurred to them. But how is it possible for the governing establishment to get the community acting in concert, in an orderly and predictable way, if it is not also thinking together and accepting the same things as right and proper?

The establishment can use both force and persuasion to that end. It can act and speak in manners designed to win over the hearts and minds of the people, or it can oblige them to toe the line and punish them if they will not. Either way, authority has always taken a not-very-benevolent interest in the media of mass communication, starting with gossip round the campfire and moving on through church sermons and political pamphlets to the newspapers and broadcasting of today. No matter how tolerant a govern-

ment may be, it eventually grows to feel misunderstood
and traduced by those who have the gift of the gab without
the mantle of responsibility. I wish to argue that journalists
actually have less power and more responsibility than is
generally realised by either side.

I have to make a personal statement here. After some
thirty-five years in the business of mass communications I
have come to believe that the influence of the media over
society is grossly exaggerated. If one flatters oneself, one
ends up feeling about as influential as Cassandra at the siege
of Troy (she was the lady who got it right, but nobody took
any notice of her): more modestly, one is lucky to say
occasionally what the public is already beginning to think
but has not quite articulated. What matters is not what we
journalists say, but what actually happens. Perhaps we are
responsible for the lighting and acoustics of the theatre, but
we do not write the play. Often I wish that people would
stop taking us so seriously and get on with living their lives
regardless – which mostly they do.

The media *mediate* – they are middlemen, they are media
of communication, which is a dreary though vital function.
If people cannot send each other messages saying what they
want and why (and negotiate a compromise if they dis-
agree), then they can only fight each other. Force is the
language of last resort which we use when we have no other
medium in common. A common language is not just a
matter of the same words, but the same logic and overtones, too. One of the causes of the Falklands War was that
neither side really understood what the other was saying;
and we in Britain frequently misunderstand what the
Arabs, the Russians or the Japanese mean, because their
language conveys a significance beyond what the dictionary
reflects. When you translate their political speech into
English, half its significance evaporates. Our own trade
union leaders, left-wing politicians and Ulster Unionists
often slip into a special code-language which is accurate

for those who habitually speak it but misleads those who d
not.

What journalists have to do – and if they fail, there i
liable to be violence – is not only to collect and deliver suc
messages but accurately translate them. Diplomats do the
same, in their specialised field, and devote much time and
trouble to doing so. Unfortunately the mass media have les
time and often less skill and they are not always helped by
those whose messages they carry. Frequently the media are
exploited as weapons in a war of nerves; sometimes they are
given meaningless verbiage masquerading as news; and
very often they are lied to. Those who complain about us
most are commonly those who need us and use us most: but
how can we publish the truth if those who know it will not
tell it? These are among the hazards of the business, but it
has to be carried on if we are not to revert to the Fall of
Babel.

Regarded in this way, as a bridge across the gulf of
misunderstanding, the role of the mass media is a very
responsible one indeed. A society which allows no such
bridge-building is in grave danger of becoming intolerant
of criticism and being led by its rulers into repression and
physical conflict. It is always a temptation to those in power
to make life easier for themselves by disciplining the nation
and suppressing the views they consider divisive. In March
1983 the Argentinian trade union movement protested
against the economic policies of the Junta by calling a
twenty-four-hours strike; to which the military regime
responded by forbidding any mention of the event by the
officially controlled media. Such a policy, however, is
short-sighted because if people cannot express their views
openly they can only express them through violence. If they
are excluded from the general debate about life, they are
forced into secret arguments which alienate them still further. The same is true of banned persons in South Africa.

Thus it seems to me the real challenge to the journalist is

not whether he is undermining the order of society, but whether he is helping people to understand one another. Is he putting himself into the position of the person he is listening to and conveying his message faithfully to those who do not understand it? The journalist must, of course, ask himself whether he is being exploited, lullabyed, lied to, for it is no part of journalism to be naïve. But the ultimate aim is to be a faithful messenger and to convey the truth however unpalatable.

But what *is* truth? as the exasperated Pilate demanded, having heard too many sides of the case. We do not know the truth of even that celebrated trial, and all too often the conscientious journalist lacks the background, the history, the inner motivations to arrive at the real truth. Journalists are often urged to 'stick to the facts', but even that is difficult enough in an age of carefully slanted statistics, official secrecy and news management. Which facts, whose facts, and how far backwards, forwards and sideways should we go to put the news in its context? The public's right to know is an American concept, not a British one. Even the House of Commons gets its answers through the protective screen of the minister: the officials behind him are very much harder to get at and their files are not for carping journalists to see. Newsmen are often slapped down with the taunt that nobody has elected them to their self-appointed posts as tribunes of the people; but then nobody has elected the civil servants, either.

Government reluctance to take the media into its confidence stems from two principal fears: that the information will be reported and exploited selectively, to the detriment of party policy; and that such heavy going will be made of it that no decision will be possible at all. The first implies that government itself is irreproachably objective, which seems unlikely, and the second that it is seldom as sure of its case as it pretends. Two lesser fears also play their part: that of giving away secrets to an enemy, and that of inhibiting frank discussion by laying it open to the public. It seems to me that nothing but good can come of frankness – protected, if need be by privilege and balanced by the right of reply – and in my experience most (though not all) of the secrets of defence and foreign policy are either not worth keeping or would be much better exposed to informed criticism. To say that journalists are not properly informed is to acknowledge that too much is withheld from them.

Admittedly I do take a rather High Church view of journalism as a vocation, a ministry of the word, a mission of understanding and peace-making. I am well aware that it is not always like that in practice, though I believe journalists do more good than they are given credit for. I am also aware that journalism does not have much of a reputation for godliness or even as a proper career for gentlemen. Among the British ruling classes there is a deep snobbishness towards the media, a prejudice that important information should be restricted to those who really understand it, and that things have never been the same since the working class became semi-literate and a semi-literate press was founded to pander to it.

As a cultural snob myself, I have some sympathy with this, though I lay the blame elsewhere: I lay it upon the British dislike of education, a dislike which permeates every class from the top down. Our upper classes specialise in something known as 'character building' (which plays a prominent role in the piecemeal training of our royal family), while the chief purpose of state education for the masses seems to be to keep them off the streets until it is time to join the dole queue. With few exceptions, the British do not really believe there is any value in learning to think and write and acquire knowledge or even skill. The worst thing you can say about an English boy – or, worse still, girl – is that he or she is 'clever': that probably means left-wing, and (like 'culture') cleverness has foreign overtones which the English detest. And so, with an under-educated people, it is only natural that we have under-educated media serving them.

At the same time, I do not think the media should be too respectable; for if we do not keep one foot in the gutter we will find ourselves coopted by the establishment, that very power-system which we have to monitor with detachment. (The same ought to be true of the Christian Church – but this is not the place for a digression on disestablishment.)

Whether journalists in Britain are sufficiently detached from the establishment has become a political and sociological question of some heat; though there are probably as many people who believe that journalists are lackeys of capitalism as there are who think we are a hotbed of crypto-communism. Journalists like to claim that proves we are nicely balanced, though, for myself, I am not so sure. However, it is not political bias that distorts our work so much as literary fashion, encouraged by our need to win audiences and readers. In particular, there is a vogue for the vocabulary of conflict and action: everything is described in terms of *clash, smash, battle, fury* and *rage*, because this is entertaining and exciting. There is nothing very compelling in a disagreement about the cost of school catering, but who could resist the headline MINISTER BLOODIED IN SCHOOL MEALS BATTLE? I suspect this kind of language has the effect of depressing the nervous while convincing the more stoic citizen that, as usual, the story is exaggerated and can be ignored.

It might look fairer to secure, by public intervention of some kind, papers that reflected all the main shades of opinion. But this would be a pity, since nobody need ever then encounter an opinion which differed from his or her own, and I fancy it would lead to more, not less, inflammatory language. The right to insert corrections or replies may be constructive – it is said to function in other countries – but it would surely make for a cumbersome and argumentative news medium and offer a poor substitute for an article that was well-researched in the first place. In any case it usually seems to me that those who complain of mis-representation both overestimate the power of the media and underestimate the importance of their own conduct.

Since, largely for economic reasons, it does not seem possible to give every shade of opinion its own outlet, our media are sprawled across the middle of the road in a way which is bound to dissatisfy the vocal minorities at either end of the spectrum, and more particularly the left, since it is both more evangelical and less endowed with money to put its case. I think the left could, in fact, try harder, but it is always too keen on becoming the masters to realise that journalists have to be the servants of their public.

The cold fact is that unless they are to become performing poodles, dancing to political tunes, the media have to identify much broader audiences and persuade them to buy the goods. Even the BBC has to behave *as if* it were com-mercial, for it dare not let its share of the audience fall much below that of its rivals if its survival is not to be questioned in parliament. It would be futile to produce a highly moral, ineffably educated paper that nobody bought: it is hard enough to keep a stupid and immoral paper afloat – the paragon would eventually go bust. No editor, not even the editor of The Times, can be under the illusion that his product is bought simply for the sake of the information it conveys. Nobody needs all the facts he prints, and some of those facts are of no real use to anybody, but all his readers want something interesting to enliven their humdrum day. In short, at a higher or lower level, they want entertain-ment. The moralist is on the wrong track if he thinks he can judge the media without bearing that in mind, for it is more important to the economics of the media than the quality of the truth they publish.

Looking at other countries it ought, surely, to be possible for a newspaper of quality to survive on a circulation of two or three hundred thousand, but in Britain it is not. Historically, advertisers have come to expect huge circulations and the printing unions have learnt that the need to maintain those figures is their opportunity to enforce their demands. Somehow the prophecies of disaster are never quite fulfilled: it cannot go on like this, we say, but it has gone on far longer than anyone expected fifteen years ago. Nevertheless, it is a fundamentally unhealthy situation. Inflation has almost priced conscientious journalism off the market: if it were not for the support of the advertisers, few readers would be ready to pay the full price of their papers. And ironically those papers which pride themselves most upon their independence and high standards are the ones which depend most upon advertising. It is the most vulgar papers which can claim to be giving their readers what they want.

Yet who can be sure, when there is really so little choice? How can people know what they want when there are so few examples of what they might have? Despite the poor quality of public education, do people really want this garish jumble of violence, triviality and sex? Leaving aside the readers, how can self-respecting journalists write such rubbish?

We can only return to the fact that our biggest-circulation papers are not meant to be new at all; they are almost *anti*-news papers, designed to take away the nasty taste of politics and economics and substitute brightness and thrills. Journalism has always catered for this, from the days of the wandering minstrel. Relatively few people feel involved in the latest diplomatic manoeuvres, but everyone likes a good story – about lovers racked by passion, the mighty fallen, the wicked unmasked, the humble come into a fortune. The essential information about the world can be picked up easily from radio and television; what most people seek in their paper is precisely what is *not* on the air – gossip, scandal, and naked ladies cocking a snook at the stuffiness of the establishment.

It may speak ill of me, but I find it hard to be shocked by the tits and bums on page three (or five, or seven, according to your tabloid). They are too soft to count as porn and too brazen to be erotic. On the whole, they are girls of the people and a surprising number of female readers apparently check upon them for reassurance about their own assets. Feminists can hardly approve, but the girls do not seem to me to be making any kind of serious statement. They make even nudity seem trivial, and it is this quality of triviality, of actually *refusing* to wield any influence, that pervades Britain's popular media. They will go where the wind blows, but they will not stand up to it or try to change its direction.

In contrast with the past, today's media are too pre-occupied with sheer production to devote much thought to manipulating the public. Given the speed and complexity of the operation, it is a marvel that any paper gets printed or any programme transmitted at all: they only happen thanks to mastery of the technical skills involved, and these are so demanding that the medium frequently becomes more significant than the message. It ain't what you say, but the way that you say it.

In many popular newspapers, clever headlines and layout mean more to the appeal of the product than the information that they convey. In television, action-packed moving pictures are more important than what really happened and why. The words themselves, which specify the pictures, become simplified for the benefit of the lowest common reader or viewer. A kind of automatic Newspeak emerges which is fast to read and to write. Pressure is intense upon journalists to deliver the news fast and first; there is seldom time or space to report most of the news with the detail it requires. Explanations are compressed into a quick label-phrase like 'left-wing extremist', 'oil-rich sheikhdom' or 'Palestine guerrilla chief'. It is a language which nobody but a journalist actually speaks, and it conjures up a special

News World of good, hard 'leads' acted out by cartoon personalities with very little background.

Journalists do, indeed, inhabit a special world: often tense and exciting, sometimes luxurious, always shared with other journalists. The competition that drives them on is largely artificial, for very few readers bother to compare newspapers to see who is ahead, but journalists take them all and are much influenced by each other. Above all, they are influenced by their immediate editor: they vie with each other to catch his eye with something more attractive, more daring than the others. Journalists do not really write for the public. They write for other journalists.

Out of this comes the mysterious News Consensus, and once again, if the individual will not make his stand against it, the system takes over and generates its own logic. If news is anything, it is that which has changed and thus become new. But at any given time some changes are thought to be more important than others. There are waves of fashion which confirm themselves as significant, because if everybody is reporting something it *must* be news.

Contrary to some complaints, news is not always bad news. One man's disaster is another man's triumph; much news is neutral; and if there really is good news, most editors are only too happy to headline it. Most of what makes me happy – flowers in the garden, a new poem, a visit from an old friend – are quite normal events which I do not expect to appear in the papers. But I do expect them to warn me if there is something unpleasant on the way.

Foreigners are a frequent source of unpleasantness because they fail to do what *we* would do, and we usually hear about them when they do things we did not expect. We might be less outraged if we understood their normal behaviour better, but normal behaviour is not news and resident foreign correspondents have become extremely expensive. It is cheaper to fly out the Fire Brigade when the action gets hot, even if they are not quite sure what is going on. The net result of this kind of adventuring is much resentment on the part of the country being attended to, and a confirmation among the British public that foreigners are, indeed, unpleasant and probably mad.

The News Consensus has been known to change its mind, however. The consensus used to be that Robert Mugabe was a particularly nasty terrorist (or was he a guerrilla or even a freedom-fighter?) Within a year it transpired that he was really a statesman in the mould of the late Jomo Kenyatta (about whom even nastier things had once been said), though a year later still there were doubts whether Mr Mugabe was not just another tribal tyrant. Then there was that jovial sergeant, Idi Amin. And the dispossessed Yasser Arafat, who was quite transformed by what the Israelis did to him in Beirut. The consensus did not approve of that at all, though it did approve of the Falklands expedition, branding the Argentinos as both unpleasant and mad.

Nearer home, much the same consensus applies to Mr Tony Benn, Mr Arthur Scargill, Mr Ray Buckton, Dr Ian Paisley, Sir Keith Joseph and Mr Enoch Powell, all but one of whom (in my experience) are both sane and pleasant. Admittedly they do not always endear themselves by the antagonising language with which they advocate their causes; they may even be wrong, though surely not all the time, and it is most unlikely they have not got what they consider good reasons for what they do. The handy consensus, though, is not that they are mistaken but that they are mad and bad, which is both unfair and unchristian. Unchristian because, under the Fatherhood of God, it must surely be a sort of blasphemy to write off our fellow men or women as less than human. If God cares for and serves them all, so should we: especially the Christian journalist.

I have already indicated that I do not think it will do to blame the News Consensus on a sinister ruling-class conspiracy of press barons and broadcasting governors. Anyone who has worked in the media knows that it is extremely rare to receive a directive to blacklist anyone. I think there is a middle-class, southeast-English bias in some organisations, which means that the working-class provincial is sometimes taken less seriously than he should be; but I think more serious is the bias against change. This may seem odd in a profession that lives by reporting change, but the media sense – correctly, in my opinion – that most of the public do not want their lives shaken up and disapprove of those who would shake them.

Perhaps it is time we all became less fearful of listening to views we do not agree with, and still less of allowing other people to hear them. If we are so sure that *we* are not deceived, why can we not trust other people's sagacity as much? Unless we can reason together we are almost bound to end up hitting each other.

So if the media want to avoid violence they should be prepared to abandon the vocabulary of conflict, stop presenting everything in terms of *crises* and *clashes*, question the consensus and allow a much wider range of views to be expressed without horror. And authority should allow such views to be aired without accusing the media of seeking to undermine society.

The media in Britain, and more especially television, stand charged with going far beyond the reporting and entertaining of society and actually moulding it. Trendiness and permissiveness (whatever they may be) are particularly laid at television's door, so are crimes of violence, the IRA, race riots, teenage sex and football hooliganism, though most of these were well established long before television and are indulged in by people who watch TV less than most of us. Television is, in fact, a rather poor way of spreading ideas and giving information: like a fireworks display, it is full of sound and fury but leaves very little specific behind. Nevertheless, because it introduces into the home, nationwide, the image of something being done it is credited with an almost supernatural influence far greater than that of any newspaper, and is thus to be controlled.

Quite apart from the question of who is to do the controlling, and with what positive aims if any, are these assumptions correct? The research that has been done into television and violence is extensive but contradictory. One of the most elaborate American surveys (that of the Surgeon General of the United States) concluded that there was a small tendency for violent television to encourage violence among the children of violent parents. But which came first: violent chicken or violent eggs? And is television the creator of a trivial, materialistic society, or could only a trivial and materialistic society have produced television? It is not surprising the argument goes round in a circle, for television is part of the *circulation* of ideas, along with books, papers, religion, art, conversation and (perhaps most important of all) observed behaviour. Television is a means of communication, not a philosophy. The ideas it communicates are abstracted from life by those who *use* television. Sometimes they are brilliant but tormented people who make programmes as a kind of personal psychotherapy, and it is my guess that such people are more influenced by books than by any other medium. But, curiously, nobody bothers about controlling books any more.

If, in criticising the media, you are criticising those who use them, then something may be achieved. For only people can be morally responsible (and responsive), not media. What I am trying to do in these chapters is to show what the pressures are upon morality in various fields of life, and why people yield to them. But I have also been arguing that there are points in everyone's life where the individual must choose to choose, choose between the pressures of the system and the demands of a moral order over and against it. Like millions before me, I feel obliged to call the source of that order God. A system, I think, does not know God.

This choosing to choose requires some courage, some effort. It means asserting our free will when it is probably easier to roll with the inertia of the situation. It means running the risk of being misunderstood and perhaps unpopular. Here the Christian believer has access both to guidance and the strength to follow that guidance, though I fancy those of us in the media do not call on them often enough and that we do not choose to say No to the system often enough.

For example, notwithstanding my levity about pinup girls, gratuitous displays of pornography and violence are wrong because they are wrong, regardless of their effect, and one must be morally dead not to know that. Whether or not they make people go off and commit rape and assault, it is an affront to the moral order to insult and demean human dignity. If that sounds a humanist way of putting it, I am happy to join hands with the humanists; but if you ask why human dignity deserves to be respected, I would say it is because human beings are designed and valued by God. Either way, Christian or humanist, we cannot trivialise humanity, we cannot refuse to take it seriously, without trivialising ourselves and abdicating our God-given freedom to choose the better and abjure the worse.

Moral issues always mean taking things seriously. Still more, they mean taking *people* seriously as equal children of God, and contemplating that deeply. That there is a Divine will for us does not mean that the right course will be obvious, for what God wants is not that we hit the bullseye for His pleasure, but that we choose, that we make the effort which shows that we care for his caring. Morally the point is not 'I think, therefore I am' but 'I choose, therefore I am', and the journalist, with his constant choice of words and images, must hold that before himself all his working day.

CHAPTER EIGHT

The God Squad

Earlier in this expedition I quoted Samuel Johnson's definition of religion: 'Virtue, as founded upon reverence of God
and expectation of future rewards and punishments.'
Although it is my argument that morality does ultimately
depend upon the will of God, I think Johnson's definition is
far too narrowly rational. What is more, it lays religion
open to discredit on the grounds that it constantly fails to
produce virtue and is apparently little more than the search
for personal advantage and the avoidance of discomfort,
even though neither of these can actually be confirmed.

Johnson's definition was born of the Age of Reason, and
as reason extends its boundaries (or so we like to think it
does) religion stands up less and less well to that kind of
scrutiny; which is hardly surprising when it is being tested
by inadequate standards. To the Christian, at any rate,
religion is more than morality or The Good. The expectation of reward or punishment fades out of mind and we can
hardly speak even of right or wrong up against the experience and knowing of God, which is what religion is finally
about. It is not about virtuous deeds, even when inspired by
reverence, but about a way of apprehending reality which is
usually described as faith.

Nevertheless, moral behaviour is not irrelevant; it is supposed to follow from faith, and the religious are justly
criticized for not doing better. If they really are religious
they will have no more bitter critics than themselves and, as
Christians, they should know how to benefit from the

process. Having turned a religious light upon various fields of worldly activity, I now want to subject religion itself, and the Christian Church in particular, to moral criticism.

It is easy to be carried away by the aesthetic experience of the Church and to confuse beauty with holiness. I was moved to tears, a few years ago, by a ceremony in Salisbury Cathedral (surely the most perfect of all the great shrines of England) to dedicate Gabriel Loire's stained glass windows in memory of prisoners of conscience. The Close at Salisbury seems to turn its back on the frenzy of the world. The spire is an impossible act of faith. The walls form a casket of prayer, in the depths of which the five lancets glow with a blue mystery that shifts and changes as you come closer, to discover that the abstract patterns are built up from scores of tiny faces just as the music that fills the vaulting is a river of tiny notes.

But I can never indulge in a purple passage like that, in the course of religious writing or broadcasting, without being brought down to earth by a salvo of letters from people who are sickened by the very mention of the Church and its glories. 'Hypocrisy!' they cry, 'Jesus told His disciples to be humble and serve the poor. Read Matthew Chapter 23: Call no man your father upon earth! Be not ye called masters! What's all this pomp and ceremony of popes and bishops – all these palaces and treasures (not forgetting the Church of England's investment portfolio and the Vatican Bank)? Sell all you have and give to the poor! And stop canting about Love Thy Neighbour: church people are as mean and selfish as anyone else.'

And there is a somewhat different flow of criticism which goes: 'Christianity is just a load of old fairy-tales and superstitions used by the ruling class to make people behave. It's just another instrument of power. It worked when folk were too ignorant to know any better and were frightened of hell fire. But now everything can be explained by science, the bottom's dropped out and the myths are exploded. Some sort of God who lets the innocent suffer! All the worst things in history were caused by your religion – wars, torture, persecutions, crusades, burning at the stake, trying to stop people finding out the truth . . . Look at Northern Ireland! We're better off without religion. Help stamp out the Church! Man is his own best friend!'

All of these things have been written or shouted at me over the past few years and they fall into two main heaps: one of those who think that Jesus had some good ideas but has been distorted and betrayed by an apostate Church, and the other of those who believe that all religion is a fraud – a dangerous fraud at that – and that if there is any power above us it is to be found in science or in the rationality of man or in the two combined as scientific humanism. To such people religion is at best outmoded, at worst a tyranny.

To take the last line of criticism first, it is necessary to form some idea of why men and women should need religion at all; for it will not hold water to argue that it is simply imposed upon them by order of the state, since religion persists in countries like Russia and China where authority is dogmatically atheist. People seem to need religion, even if that does not prove that what they get is necessarily true.

I have met at least two scientists – Professor Sir Alister Hardy, the Oxford zoologist, and Professor P. J. Lachmann, the Cambridge immunologist whose bee-thesis I quoted earlier – who argue that the religious instinct is one of man's greatest evolutionary advantages, enabling him to adapt to situations which would otherwise have defeated him. Hardy emphasises the inner comfort and strength which religion brings; Lachmann, who is more sceptical, emphasises the moral discipline involved, regardless of whether the underlying stories are true or false. What both professors are saying is that religion is in fact useful, not detrimental, to our welfare, and I can only repeat that far from undermining our trust in God this only confirms the Christian view of His love for us. The theories we construct about Him cannot possibly be more than partial truths, always open to development, but they cannot alter the nature of what He does and is. What most of us mean by 'God', most of the time, is a limited construction imposed upon the limitless, because we cannot talk about or even contemplate the limitless Itself. Yet we are aware of It, that It is in us and yet other than us, that It cares about us, and that It is the ultimate reality in that everything only makes sense in relation to It. We cannot *prove* this without destroying Its voluntary nature, and so it is necessary that – as we strip off more and more of the magic and mumbo-jumbo which are not of Its essence – there should be increasing numbers of people who doubt Its very existence in traditional religious terms. Hence it is not uncommon, in my experience, to be told, vehemently, that I cannot possibly believe in the sort of God which I do not think we have anyway.

There can be no doubt that primitive religion had a large content of magic and mumbo-jumbo, of attempts to explain what could not be understood and to manipulate the laws of nature, most of which has been stripped away by the methods of science. But all this tells us is that God is not an arbitrary potentate pulling strings for His favourites. The more we learn about *how* things work, the more we are driven towards the awesome question *why*? Nor is it enough for most people with any depth of being to content themselves with the conclusion that things simply *are*, that they have no other meaning in relation to some ultimate reality and that the best we can do is to enjoy ourselves and behave reasonably; for either we find ourselves bitterly disappointed at the fraudulence of life, or we devise language to satisfy our need to speak *as if* there were some deeper reality. What very few people do, in my experience, is to behave as if life were totally absurd.

The advance of psychiatry has raised the theory that religion is really neurotic in origin and that far from being an insight into reality it is an escape from it on the part of those who cannot face the hard facts. Or, just as an infant seeks the love and protection of its parents, the infantile part of the adult yearns for a Father in Heaven and experiences the same feelings of guilt towards Him as it did towards its parents in childhood. As for the Church and its clergy – all those men with all that power over all those women – they are full of sexual symbolism and every kind of Freudian kink from transvestism to sublimated homosexuality.

In which there is a good deal of truth, just as one can make Freudian readings of the armed forces, trade unionism and the English public schools system. Some of the oddities, like male domination, are inexcusable and overripe for reform. Others ought to be tolerated, for homosexuals and celibates often make devoted priests, as they do school-teachers; while others again are quite naturally expressive of the human condition and none the worse for that. To insist that modern man must have no ritual, no symbolism, no echoes of the magical past is to underestimate the depth of his spirit and leave a vacuum which will surely be filled by something less tried and tested. To feel *unforgivably* guilty before God is to betray a serious misunderstanding of the Christian faith; but for a grown person to seek the for-giveness of the Heavenly Father, far from being infantile or neurotic, is mature and extremely healthy. It is those who can find no such reconciliation who risk breakdown.

From the dismissal of religion that one hears from secu-larists one would imagine that faith appealed solely to ignorant mad old ladies, which is simply not true. Old ladies there may be – I suspect women in general are spiritually more sensitive than men – but I find them no more ignorant or mad than those who never go to church at all. The work of the Religious Experience Unit at Oxford and Nottingham indicates that a knowledge of God is far more widespread than most people suppose, and that those who have such knowledge are, if anything, better educated and less neurotic than the median. Whether they find anything relevant to their experience in the Church is another, very serious, matter. My point is here that to be a sane, male scientist in your fifties is evidently no barrier to believing in God.

I am well aware that I could stand accused of believing in religion because I want to believe in religion – and I do want to, for several reasons. As I look at the world around me, the things I see and hear, the events that happen to me and the sensations that come over me, I recognise certain patterns, I feel certain currents and attractions, which hang together in a mysterious way, which seem to make sense outside the physical chain of cause and effect. Why, for example, am I wrestling with these words now, struggling to say something which I know cannot be said? I can only say that something is calling me to say it, and for Its purposes rather than mine. Unless I have the *language* of religion and can call that It God, I can get no further. I am aware that this language is inadequate, that it is only a set of tools to work with and not the Thing Itself, but once I begin to use it, my experiences of life start to make sense and I am a great deal less confused and frustrated than I was. I need religion, and for me it works. Yet it is not merely self-fulfilling, because I find that as I work with it it leads me down unexpected paths to discoveries which I did not particularly want. For example, five years ago I never imagined I could have any use for the idea of the Trinity; but now, despite some of its crudities, I find it central and fascinating.

I want religion, also, because knowing human nature as I do I distrust the notion of 'every man his own church': in short, I want organised religion, and I think this as necessary as organised liberty in the political field. I think we must all have a personal experience of God, and I am not

ashamed to say I have mine – moments of intense awareness
of being loved, a compelling phrase burning into my head –
but I am convinced that if we relied solely upon our private
revelations, our religious life would be sad, mad and
ultimately bad. We must check our revelations against the
wisdom of the past if they are not to remain selfish and
probably very shallow. Which is not to say we must swal-
low every dogma the Church teaches; the Church itself is
developing, slowly, all the time, chivvied and buffeted by
its critics; but the critics, too, must prove their case against
the orthodox. There has to be some intellectual rigour,
some discipline, if the religious-minded are not to be
isolated from one another and picked off by those who seek
power for its own sake.

I want religion because it offers an alternative source of
criticism to secular power, and an alternative community.
The Church fails all the time to be the community it was
meant to be, for in so many ways the secular state has
appropriated its functions: yet it is genuinely good that we
should gather together with neighbours we have not chosen
and acknowledge that we *are* one body and that our duty is
not just to save our own souls but to care for one another
here and now. Outside our very limited families, where else
do we do that today? In our businesses, in our trade unions,
our political parties? In a worshipping congregation we are
reminded to love those against whom we may be going on
strike next week.

Finally I want religion because I think it is very hard to
gain access to God without the opportunity it provides. I
am sorry to say this, in a way, because if the religious claim
is true it ought to permeate the whole of life without any
special occasions. Knowing God, recognizing the reality of
the world, should be continuous; by setting it apart in
special buildings at special times the Church is cutting
people off from religion, making it something for members
only.

But the fact is, because we are fallen and wilful and know it, we cannot bear to live all the time in the way of holiness. We crowd God out with busy-ness and distraction, we explain Him away with partial truths, and the Church has had to salvage what it can and preserve it in a museum where it no longer applies to the world outside. Hindus, Muslims and Buddhists still manage to keep a fair amount of religion in their daily lives. They have to, in order to make sense, for they have not yet learnt to devise artificial lives detached from God. They still do religion in the streets, where it belongs.

And yet even the oriental faiths do have their ceremonies and temples set apart, for they also are fallen and sinful and have to make a special effort to re-connect themselves with the Father. The practice of organized religion puts one in the mood to make that effort; it concentrates the mind and presents the ikon through which the eye can pass 'and then the heavens espy'. If one does not learn these techniques and the language that goes with them in some sort of temple ceremony, the chances are today that one will never learn them elsewhere.

That the languages are there at all suggests to me that they have something to say or they would not have been developed. To some they take the form of hermeneutics (the interpretation of scripture), to others the metalanguage of the sacraments, and to others like myself the mystical language of contemplation which is more a matter of listening than of talking back. Put them all together and the religious approach appears as not just another dimension but as something three-dimensional in itself. That it has something in common with art is not surprising, for art is an attempt to *express* the same reality in sensuous terms, encompassing its own trinity of unity, movement and harmony. One would expect to find such activity drawn to the presence of the Godhead; but it is, further, the finest gift that the human spirit can make to its origin. All art is a form of thanksgiving, a way of saying: 'We give thanks for this aspect of reality in your gifts to us.'

There remains the humanist criticism, that religion seeks to ascribe to God the love and the values that are really due to humanity itself; and since God does not exist, religion is really an attempt to purloin those honours for the Church and thereby acquire power for the clerical elite (of whom humanists are often ambivalently contemptuous and jealous).

I do not intend to spare the rod to the Church or the clergy, but it seems to me that they have served mankind far better than any abstract humanism. Priest and presbyter may have twisted the Gospel to unworthy ends but they have at least some traditional restraints, some pattern of discipline to contain their pride, whereas the humanist leader has nothing but the fashionable definition of which group of his friends really counts as human and in what direction it should be moving. I am inclined to think that the Church, and more especially the protestant churches, has made too much of the incurable sinfulness of man and the helplessness of our wills. But I think the history of mankind over the past two centuries (and longer, if you will) does not suggest that we become more dignified and humane the less we listen to religion. I would be prepared to bet that more millions have gone to a miserable death in the name of the Reich or the People's Revolution than were slaughtered in the name of the cross or the crescent.

Humanists may say that they, too, reject the counterfeit religions of Fascism and Communism, and that what they aspire to is a world governed by reason, which eschews violence and respects the sanctity of human life and the dignity of the individual. But there are two basic flaws in this apparently virtuous attitude. The first is that it leaves a God-shaped hole in the human spirit, a hole which is liable to be filled not by an image of universal Humanity but of 'Our Kind of Man' in comparison with whom the rest are damned. The most ominous example of this is to be found in the philosophy of Nietzsche, the father of Nazism.

Nietzsche maintained that the one great freedom was freedom from God. To him the Good was everything that heightened the feeling of power in man; the Bad was every form of weakness, especially Christian self-sacrifice which he saw as no better than suicide. Reaching back to Hegel, Nietzsche conjured up a higher type of man, the Superman, and claimed that Christianity, with its exaltation of the weak, had constantly sought to undermine such beings by debauching the intellect with notions of pity, meekness and forgiveness. It was all a Jewish trick to survive at all costs. 'How a German could ever have felt Christian is beyond me!', he exploded, 'I condemn Christianity on the most terrible charge any prosecutor has ever made . . . The Church has left nothing untouched by its depravity. It has made a lie of every truth.' This worship of power, this hatred of gentleness, pointed towards war as the one great climax in life where the Superman could realize his potential and enjoy his freedom to the full. Thus we see how Nietzsche's humanism set Europe on the road to Stalingrad and Auschwitz.

The second flaw in civilized humanism is that in the end neither man nor woman can be trusted to remain virtuous and reasonable, even if virtue is to be defined purely by reason. For reason is corruptible and it is not, in any case, a sufficient guarantee of virtue. It is corruptible both literally, because there are so many subtle pressures upon us, and because we cannot always be sure that it is fully informed. It is not an adequate guarantee of the right choice because the mere logic of the equation need take no account of the vital moral determinant 'What sort of person do I think I am?' The religious person should know himself to be designed by God not merely to preserve his own dignity or to respect the sanctity of his own life – or yet his concept of the dignity and sanctity of others – but to love and glorify the loving

God. The sort of person he is will be constructed out of countless choices of this kind, all of them made in relation to the reality of God.

And so we come to the more specific charge against religion as most of us know it: that the Christian Church has betrayed its trust and is now apostate, a traitor to its Lord.

There must be very few visitors who can browse round an ancient cathedral without the uneasy feeling that Jesus Christ would have been in trouble there. There are not actually money-changers or animals for sale in the cloisters, but there is usually a postcard stall or souvenir shop of some kind, a strong hint that you are expected to pay to walk round, and extra charges to climb the tower or inspect the vestments and the treasury. Even the tombs make it more like a Hall of Fame than a House of Prayer.

As for the structure itself: maintaining a place like Salisbury is like painting the Forth Bridge when it is seven hundred years old. You can well understand why it costs a fortune, but the question is whether the Church should have allowed itself to become a museum-keeper or a branch of the National Trust when the instructions of its Founder were to get out and about preaching the will of God and serving the poor, the sick and the imprisoned. How did it happen – this vast empire of property and administration, this accumulation of sterile wealth, this career structure for men dressed up as women (but on no account women dressed up as men)?

Whatever became of the simple Gospel: repent of your sins, love your neighbour, share a little bread and wine in remembrance of Me? How did it happen – all this turgid liturgy, revised prayer-books, arguments about the Trinity and who cannot share communion with whom? It all seems to have become a game for its own sake, not only remote from the life of Jesus but just as remote from the lives of people today.

There are some practical excuses to be made first. The

Church exists, it is an historical fact, and like the heir to a stately home it has to decide whether to keep the place going, sell it for some other use or allow it to fall into ruins. There are very few people indeed who would opt for ruins: the tourist traffic, if nothing else, bears witness to that. As for a change of use, who wants a cathedral? What other purpose could it possibly serve? Even if it is no more than a museum, at least it manages to support itself, one way or another, without running to the state for subsidy. (This is not quite true today, now that the state is making grants towards the preservation of historical churches, but whether you see that as a recognition of the tourist attraction or as a payment for spiritual and aesthetic services rendered it has come pretty late in the day.)

The Church itself groans under the weight of its inheritance. It could do a much more cost-effective job of spreading the Gospel without its Norman pillars and Gothic arches, for they are not only extravagant but mostly in the wrong places, entrenched in the county towns instead of the suburbs and industrial areas. But you cannot move them; and you cannot, either, ignore two things – that people love them dearly, if for all the wrong reasons, and that past generations of believers have made unsheddable investments in them both of treasure and of prayer. Few Christians today with some thousands of pounds to spare would put it into a shrine rather than a working charity; but in the past they saw otherwise, and they wished to honour God by providing Him with palaces at least as splendid as those of the princes of the earth. They were not so simple as to imagine that God actually needed such palaces to live in, but they did believe that things – even buildings – could express more than words could say; and having made those expressions they drenched them in worship and prayer which does not easily wash off. A cathedral like Salisbury is not just an out-of-date and inconvenient building, or a work of art; it is a permanent offering, a standing prayer, and it would be an arrogant insult to our forefathers to let it fall down. If the Church means anything it means continuity; and to be the heirs to a continuous prayer, seven hundred and more years old, ought to make us at least respectful of that inheritance. There may be things we can learn from it that are not dreamed of in our philosophy.

Certainly there are other ways we could pay for it. We could, like some European countries, levy a church tax, turn priests into state employees and nationalize the church investments. Quite apart from betraying the intentions of those who left their money to the Church, I doubt whether either the Church or the taxpayers would welcome that. Relations between Church and State are delicate enough without having to go through the files of a Ministry for Religion.

The classic explanation for the worldliness of the Church is that the rot set in when the Emperor Constantine abandoned the gods of Rome and adopted Christianity as the official religion of the Empire. There are some reasons for doubting the sincerity of Constantine's conversion: for one thing, he needed the allegiance of the Christians in his army, and for another he needed an ideology which would consecrate his rule in a way that would impress the Greeks and Asians. As the centuries went by, the state became increasingly dependent upon the Church for its administration and propaganda, and the Church was richly rewarded for its services. Personally, I cannot blame the Church for seizing its opportunities and persuading itself that it was harnessing the State to God's purposes rather than being taken for a ride in the opposite direction. There was the example of the Old Testament to suggest how kings and priests could coexist in one holy nation.

It is true that the Church of the Apostles could never have intended such a coalition, but then the Church of the Apostles almost certainly expected an apocalypse long before that became imaginable. The Church which came to power some three hundred years after the death of Christ found itself in a position never remotely contemplated by the gospels. It had developed far beyond the fellowship of the apostles even before Constantine adopted it. Yet it would be futile of us to pretend that our duty was to take it back to the beginning again, since our very understanding of the faith, and to some extent the very texts of scripture that we use, are not as they were at the beginning, but have been conditioned by the intervening centuries. If there has been a 'betrayal' it is inscrutable, inevitable and providential. Without it no sort of Christianity would have survived to our day at all. Yes, man has bent the faith to his purposes, which have not always been worthy; but since the faith is God's gift for our use, can it be God's intention that it be rendered useless by change of circumstances? There is bound to be compromise, and I am surprised how much of the original faith (so far as we can still sense it) has survived.

Often the compromise has been disgraceful. Far too often the Church has compromised with Nietzsche's Superman, blessing his wars, acquiescing in his freedom from God, looking tolerantly upon his contempt for weakness, pity and forgiveness. This is precisely when worldly authority has found the Church a loyal ally and its intervention in politics entirely acceptable; for the fact is that while the world chides the Church for failing to live up to its Gospel it is a gospel in which the world itself does not really believe. Wistfully the world sometimes dreams of a society in which the weak receive justice and the scars of sin are healed by forgiveness, but it does not really believe it would work unless everyone could be compelled to act so. The point is, however, not whether it will work but whether it is right, and that is a leap which authority never dares take for fear of losing its authority.

Chistians should know this, but in practice they are no more likely to follow it than anyone else; for they live (as is often said) in two worlds, the world of the spirit and the world of the flesh. There are certain dangers in chopping life in half like this: both worlds belong to God and both are susceptible to sin, but the world of the spirit is private and easy to overlook, while the world of the flesh is public and impossible to ignore. Christians would say it was somehow an expression of the spirit and to be treated as such, but their understanding of this is difficult and often lacks conviction. Believers as well as non-believers find it easier to yield to the logic of worldly systems than to challenge them with the Will of God. Christians generally are as sinful as the rest.

And that is why they are in church. The Church is not a congregation of the good – it is an assembly of the sinful who know that they are sinful and seek to do something about it. They have little confidence in their own capacities, but as Christians they believe that *God*, as Christ, has done something about it. But just what?

To answer that question would take several more books, and even then it would not be answered because either I should have expounded one particular form of Christianity and would have to defend myself against the others, or I should have summarized half a dozen schools of theology and left the reader to make his own choice. I should only have confirmed that Christianity is divided and uncertain and that it has, above all, frustrated its Master's prayer – 'that they all may be one'.

I know what I myself believe: that even if Jesus was not God – He is now; and that He is an irresistible sign to us of the way God is, suffering with us and like us, yet forgiving and rising again, crucified hour after hour, resurrected day after day. I cannot see any other way of coping with our endless failure, any other tincture or catalyst that will resist the corrosion of sin and evil. This may sound vague, but to me it is very deep and I sense that in this we *are* all one if only we will quieten ourselves, go down deep into the silence together where we can meet the God we all share within us, and let Him speak, not us.

It is when we become too talkative and start trying to define parts of God, trying to persuade or bully each other to accept our own limited views of Him, that the trouble begins. We have different temperaments, different experiences of life, different wounds and hungers: how then should exactly the same faith be appropriate to us all. How could a loving Father be so lacking in discrimination among us? Each of us stands in a different spot; how can we all have the same view? Each of us has a part of the whole: how can we appreciate the full glory unless we allow them all to come together without excluding any that is true to its own viewpoint?

Even this is too static a simile, for we are all on the move, singly and as communities. Faith must develop and change as all things must to stay alive; but slowly, organically, never betraying its true nature, though its leaves and flowers may surprise us with their changes.

So do we just contemplate the tree in silence? Some do, and that is enough for them. Most of us, less solitary, want to talk about it, discuss and understand it, even celebrate and decorate it, for that is human nature. We are constantly striving to make sense, even when it is beyond our understanding to do so. But we must never deceive ourselves that all our busy-ness about the tree really *is* the tree. All our words about God are not God.

So for some of us, including myself a lot of the time, the Church gets in the way of God. It tries to put Him in a gilded cage and fence Him in with words and ceremonies and hang a label on the fence reading 'GOD (*Deus Optimus Maximus*). Male. Trinitarian. Inhabits ancient buildings. Feeding time: Sunday 1130 (by ticket only).' But the cage is empty.

I am less than fair. Sometimes a glittering form is glimpsed high among the vaulting. But I believe the Holy Spirit is more often to be seen in the mundane plumage of a sparrow in the streets outside than as an exotic firebird within. If there is a God who presented Himself to us in the form of a Galilean carpenter's son who could be mistaken for a gardener, a stranger on the road or by the lakeshore, then He is likely to be a far more common experience than we wish to recognize.

The Christian Church's God is out-of-date and remote because we wish Him to be so and have made Him so. The Church itself is quaint and hierarchical because its followers do not really want it otherwise. They do not want it to burst its ancient walls and flood the streets because they know how very uncomfortable and demanding that would be. It must stay out of their homes, out of their work-places and their politics, because if it ever got in they would have to change. I do not call them hypocrites, because, as I have said before, the one hypocrisy is to accuse others of it; but I would urge them to note one more sign. In a corner of the Close at Salisbury stands a figure of the Virgin by Elizabeth Frink. She is no tender maiden stooped in adoration, but a woman weathered by suffering, striding out, away from the great church.

CHAPTER NINE

Enjoy, Enjoy!

My last chapter was fairly strenuous going; penitential, perhaps. The moral and religious life is not really bound to be joyless – I know plenty of men and women who live it joyfully – but deep within most of us lies the gloomy conviction that being good and God-fearing rules out having fun. This is partly the fault of the Church, with its ancient heresy that whatever delights the flesh must distract the soul from total devotion to God. We are told that God manifests Himself to us in His earthly gifts; but have not the holiest people denied themselves every bodily comfort to reach the heights? Their example has entrenched the belief that the religious life must be set apart from the world, a rigour which most of us do not want and could not manage if we wished it, because of our responsibilities to others. Partly also our conviction does reflect our awareness that we are sinful and that many of the things that please us will turn out wrong. We might do better if we chose to; but choosing can be tiresome and so we slip into the assumption that morality brings misery and that pleasure lies outside it.

This is very poor theology. If we believe in a Creator God, it hardly seems likely that He will have endowed us (and the innocent beasts) with pleasant sensations which are inherently evil. Even the sense of having done right is a pleasure. It is our motive for seeking these pleasures and the use we make of them – in two words, our choice – that raises the moral issue and the possibility of unhappiness.

Pleasure is transmitted through the nervous system and

registered in the brain, but it is commonly stimulated by things; and in our society access to things costs money. It is not just a matter of being able to buy and possess works of art, food, clothes, wine and video-cassettes: simply to live and be able to walk down the street enjoying the scene and the people we meet costs money. The law of diminishing returns applies: I doubt if the person with five hundred pounds a week enjoys ten times as much pleasure as the person with fifty; but there is clearly a level below which there is little if any pleasure to be had, and that level seems to be rising all the time. For better or worse, we are a consumer society, a society which gets most of its pleasant rewards from buying and using things, services as well as goods, though the goods are the most obvious and enviable.

Have we gone too far? To be pleased may not in itself be wrong; but have we become obsessed with private satisfaction to the point where we ignore the needs of our less fortunate neighbours, neglect our own moral and spiritual natures, and allow the system which satisfies our demands to grind its way over creation, devouring man and nature as it goes?

The past quarter century illustrates the dilemma into which the juggernaut has driven itself. On the one hand, the realization that it was poisoning the globe, burning up its resources and widening the gap between the living standards of the rich nations and the poor. On the other, the realization that if the juggernaut slowed down things would get even worse for the poor while the rich thrashed wildly about trying to keep their balance.

No sooner have we developed a sense of guilt about our extravagance than we are urged to spend more so that the unemployed can go back to making us luxuries. Must it be luxuries? Can it not be constructive goods and services for those who really need them? But the world is now so complex and so interconnected, politically as well as economically, that nobody seems able to devise a system which will work on the basis of the rich giving to the poor and receiving little or nothing in return. It is not just that the rich are greedy. Some cannot help making money, any more than a musician can help making music. Others are generous, others simply careless. The system itself depends upon the recirculation of wealth, and nobody can be certain that the destruction involved in tearing the system down and building anew can be survived. Multinational capitalism may, as they say, have been built on their deathpits.

No one of conscience can avoid doubts of this kind, but they have a strong element of self-flagellation: it may be good for the soul but contributes nothing to the community. The Christian who lives in the here and now as comfortably as I do is likely to find himself confronting the moral dilemmas of the Consumer Society in much more seductive terms: say, the splendours of Harrods or Fortnum and Mason, of a well-stocked wine merchant or a great restaurant, all purveyors of no mere necessities but explicit pleasures. Can we honestly sit back and enjoy them, knowing what we should about our faith and our fellow men?

I might excuse myself, as I tuck in to the *canard sauvage* or adjust my Cashmere dressing-gown, with the thought that I have worked hard and deserve some pleasant reward at last; that beside my lofty intellect and my spiritual sensibility there is, within me, a little boy begging for a treat, whom I cannot put down for ever. I might even argue that my purchase will put money into circulation and stimulate employment; for surely the worst thing I could do would be to keep my earnings in my pocket where they would do no good to anyone. Admittedly I could do more for the unemployed by ordering a house or a ship to be built for me; but I already have a house and feel no need for a ship. My essential needs are already satisfied: I have two pairs of shoes, three indifferent suits, a hat, a raincoat and an umbrella. The government taxes me as it wills and I make my donations to charity. Surely it is not *wicked* of me to take pleasure in this lawfully-gotten duck or dressing gown? Or is it? For I could very well survive without either and send the money to Oxfam or Cafod or Tearfund or Christian Aid.

The standing-ground from which we make our moral decisions is our response to the question – What sort of person do I think I am? What am I made, meant to be or wish to be? For I am trying, now in my middle-age, to live up to some consistent pattern which I can manage and which those I care about will recognize and respect. I suppose that if I had identified myself as a monk I would be governing my behaviour by the Rule of St Benedict, and be looking to my fellow monks for confirmation that I was making the grade, regardless of what milkmen or insurance agents might think. But since I have come to the conclusion that my calling is to be a journalist – a vocation which requires me to live alongside all sorts and conditions of people – I am very reluctant to depart from the ways in which most people live. That still leaves me plenty of room to make moral choices, but I do not feel obliged to adopt certain disciplines of behaviour – poverty, celibacy, regular offices and fasting – which would make me appear to be more dedicated than I am. However serious I may be about being a Christian, I am not prepared to take it to the point of breaking my fellowship with my colleagues, friends and family and making myself a stranger to them. I know I am no different from them, and I believe that if God has any service for me to render then it will be at our common level and not from me 'above' to them 'below'. Any form of service to God which was not rendered to Him *in* my fellow men would seem to be dubiously Christian. At the risk of sounding antinomian, I find it important to remain in solidarity with sinners, and not to become a holy man. Such are my lame excuses for carrying on with the *canard sauvage*.

The excuses will not be good enough for puritans, who

will protest that Jesus lived a homeless and simple life, a poor man in opposition to the rich. But that is not so clearcut as is commonly supposed. Jesus appears to have come from a respectable artisan family – small builders – and to have owned His own house at Capernaum for some time. He only embraced the life of a wandering preacher, living off hospitality, towards the end of His life and by His own choice. In contrast with John the Baptist He was not noted for asceticism. On the contrary, Jesus entertained 'publicans and sinners', stood loosely to the Law on feeding, fasting and Sabbath observance, and was regarded by some of his critics as a glutton and a drunkard. Smears those may have been, but Jesus was clearly no kill-joy; and if He held out little hope for the rich it was not on grounds of envy or class-warfare, but because the encumbrance of their property made them fail to recognize their duty to God through the poor.

More excuses. But what about the early church of Jerusalem, selling all their possessions and holding everything in common? Were they not faithfully following the teachings of their Lord? It seems to me that what they were doing made sense in terms of an oppressed community awaiting the Day of Judgment, just as it made sense for Jesus's original band of missionaries. But as the decades passed without the Last Judgment, as church membership grew and its structure became formalized, this simple communism could not possibly survive. A church which had begun as a lifeboat for a select few hoping to escape from the world was obliged to find accommodation for everyone, including a vast majority with no inclination to escape at all. Call it compromise or even corruption of the faith, but there can be no going back to the lifeboat now; or not until, once again, there remains a faithful few with Judgment Day on the horizon. Till then, the Church cannot do its work in the world if it is seen to be rowing away from it.

But if compromised Christians, which most of us are, no

longer feel the need to be beggar-poor, it does not follow that it is right for them to be stinking rich. (The rich, in fact, seldom stink: they are more likely to smell of Chanel or deodorant.) The mediaeval Church, even though it was irretrievably coopted by the Establishment, constantly reminded people of their duty to the poor in the form of charity and conjured up the Seven Deadly Sins including the loathsome figures of lust, gluttony and avarice. As I guessed earlier, the mediaeval Church can have had little chance to over-indulge – the opportunities today are much greater for all – but to those who had the opportunities the message was clear that the good things of life must not be overdone, must not be allowed to become idols in themselves. Everything in moderation.

In the days when the Church was part of the Establishment there was some hope of keeping pleasures under control by incorporating them into religious life. Music, drama, even feasting and fairing were fitted into the church calendar and the pulpit kept up a running commentary on everything from sexual morals and dress to money-lending. Now there is no such framework confining the exercise of pleasure, and the danger is that pleasure becomes an end in itself and the systems which promote it will simply maximize their profits, subject only to civil legislation. Such legislation often coincides to a large extent with what the Church would teach, but nowadays it is more concerned with maintaining law and order and protecting public health than with reminding those who can afford to buy pleasant non-essentials that they have a duty towards those who have not even the essentials. Perhaps every big store and smart restaurant should be obliged to maintain a Christian Aid collector at the door, or to levy a poor tax on all who enter.

It is very hard, though, not to be grateful for many of the products of the Consumer Society even when, strictly, one could do without them. I could have written this book in longhand instead of by typewriter, but my publisher could never have deciphered the manuscript; and I could have made my copies with economical carbon paper instead of by photocopier, but corrections are so much easier to make with the latter. My wife could do the family washing by hand and clean the house with mop and broom, but then she would have no time for her creative work as an artist. I am attentive to the arguments for wholefood, homespun and live music; but I still give thanks for frozen vegetables, wash-and-wear shirts and digital recordings. It is possible that if my wife and I renounced these modern advantages we would be worthier, healthier people in some sense: labour-saving devices often result in our having to do more labour in the end; but they do at least enable us to concentrate more of our energy on what we do best, and we hope that what we do is to the service of our fellow human beings and the glory of God.

So we hope. But whereas simple things have simple effects, the more complicated they become the more unexpected their side-effects. It is hard to think what harm a broom could do from its birth as a pole in a thicket to its retirement as a support for one of my sunflower plants. But a vacuum cleaner has an ancestry of mining and pollution and a life dependent on the burning of fossil fuels to provide electricity for it. Even the excuse that its manufacture provides work for my brothers in Scotland (or more probably Korea) has worn out, because more and more of them are being replaced by robots and the more gadgets there are in my house, the higher the unemployment rate seems to rise.

Perhaps I have concentrated too much on relatively useful goods when I should have directed my moral criticism at luxuries. The dividing line is not obvious, though. Is a car a luxury, on the grounds that we could replace it with public transport or at least with something far less fancy and extravagant than the average family saloon; or is it a real necessity for life in the urbanized West? To some degree both are true: necessities have become increasingly luxurious, as manufacturers strive to gain the advantage by arranging that what we have to have also gives pleasure. From the aesthetic point of view there should be nothing wrong in that – better a beautiful broom than an ugly one. But assuming that all cars are capable of taking us from A to B and back, people tend to look for further attractions like impressive lines, dashing performance and clever accessories which are not strictly necessary for the job but which reflect on the competence and success of the owner. There is no need here to enlarge upon the way cars transform the personalities of their drivers once they are at the wheel. Insidiously, the products of the Consumer Society not only *do something for* their purchasers but *say something about* them to other purchasers. To the competition of the manufacturers in adding pleasure to usefulness is added the competition of the consumers in showing off. Their purchases become a way of showing others 'the sort of person I am', and thus begin to have subtly moral implications.

In principle this is not new. For example, people have always expressed their relationship to money, their class and religious attitudes by the way they dress or furnish their houses. But today this sign language has been developed and speeded up by advertising through the mass media. Five years ago, successful people in my neighbourhood drove Rovers: today they are all in Volvos, and it seems to have little to do with the relative merits of the cars.

I am no great car-lover myself. Perhaps I have other ways of impressing people, or perhaps I simply lack the machismo. In any case, speed gives me an increasing sense of danger and I do not care how long it takes to get from 0 to 60 provided my car arrives at my destination without going wrong. Anyone can overtake me without my ill will, and I will concede that your car is shinier than my car without bothering to come and look: I know that mine was last washed three months ago. In other words, cars give me no pleasure. This may be a kind of inverted snobbery, but it still demonstrates how the possession of things can lead us into the clutches of pride.

The language of clothing I can understand a little more easily, if only because I am perfectly well aware that the sloppy way I dress is intended to say that I am the sort of person who does not care and does not need to care. The people whose opinion matters to me already know what I am capable of. I can see that expensive clothes may be better value for money up to a point, but I am shocked at the idea of paying two-hundred pounds for a suit when I can get something that more or less fits for seventy. Of course, I do not have to look at me. Even so, I would feel guilty (or to be more honest, resentful) at carrying a small fortune around on my carcase when the difference could have gone on books or a holiday or several bottles of Islay malt whisky. We all have our extravagances, our different sources of pleasure. The very best things in life may be free – a spring morning, the glow of affection among old friends – but they are by-products of living which cannot be bought to order. When one needs a pleasure one frequently has to buy it – and then defend it; or if one cannot afford to buy it there follows envy of those who can. The true ascetic who has renounced all possessions is free of both those forms of anxiety. Those of us who have to have things can never be.

And I come back to that little boy inside, whimpering for a treat. Perhaps he is not so infantile after all. Perhaps he only wants what is due to him: not just a bribe, but some self-respect. To be seen in a well-cut suit or a decent car or a good restaurant may not merely be to show off; it may also indicate that I refuse to patronize rubbish, and that I have my standards and do not intend to lower them. If everyone were content with cheap off-the-peg suits, old bangers and factory-made pasties, we would soon find ourselves in a shabby and shoddy society and not one, I suspect, in which the poor or the Third World would find themselves better off.

There is a case to be made that the well-to-do (among nations as well as among individuals) pioneer, with their extravagance, the goods and services which eventually benefit everyone else, and that without them the advances would either not be made or long delayed. Perhaps it ought not to be so. Perhaps such pioneering ought to be done by state institutions and international agencies on behalf of the people, but it has seldom worked that way. From hygienic sewerage down to bicycles, aluminium pots and reliable watches, not to mention the music of Beethoven and the paintings of Rembrandt, there is a huge list of blessings which would have been withheld from us all if it had not been for the pleasure of the well-to-do.

Before the rich embrace me and the poor lynch me I must go on to say that wealth does not necessarily make people good; in fact some of the most detestable people I know are very rich, though you might think they had little cause to be so disagreeable. As Jesus knew, wealth and its worries can shut off the rich from their fellow men and from perceiving God. I have met disagreeable poor people, too; but they had more excuse for their hostility and bitterness. When all is said and done, goodness can be found anywhere on the scale, irrespective of income.

What the gospels tell us is that the rich man has a heavy responsibility to serve those who are less fortunate, and that the closer he comes to God the more he will find demanded of him. Jesus's challenge to the rich was a kind of invitation to bankruptcy, and He knew that few would have the trust in Him to accept it. Apart from anything else, most owners of wealth regard themselves as holding it not just for their own use but for their families, and Jesus knew that nobody who kept their family ties could follow Him all the way. I have to admit that I cannot, and I do not think my motives are all selfish. But then our modern puritan would point out that while we might not be doing what we ought not to have done, we were probably leaving undone something that we ought to be doing.

We can't win. The blackmail of our sins of omission hangs over every Christian, and to make matters worse it is there in the Gospel: 'Inasmuch as ye did it not to one of the least of these, ye did it not to Me.' So there I sit, eating my wild duck, when I might have been visiting a hospital or a prison or sorting out unwanted clothing for the survivors of an earthquake. If I work eight hours a day, eat or sleep eight hours, there should still be eight hours when I could, in theory, be occupied in charity. Such charitable work as I do is plainly not enough, and if I gave up drinking, eating out and going to the opera I could multiply my donations many times over.

I suspect that many of us become so agonised about where to stop that we never really start, or else comfort ourselves with the thought that nowadays the government takes care of charity by redistributing part of our income through the tax and welfare system or as development aid. If that does not satisfy we can still go on, voluntarily, to adopt the discipline of tithing – setting aside as much as ten or as little as one per cent of our income for charity. Then at least we may content ourselves that we have met some definite demand. But even that was not good enough for Jesus, who refused to leave the consciences of the well-to-do in peace, and we know it is not good enough for the Third World whose needs are insatiable, a bottomless pit swallowing up everything we pour into it. Surely the price of one wild duck is not going to make any difference? Or if the duck is too blatant, who will grudge me the uplifting experience of a ticket to *The Dream of Gerontius* (a cunning alternative, this, since – though they give me equal pleasure – good music is regarded as morally worthier than good food)?

A sternly moral government would curtail our extravagances by some sort of rationing, as it did during World War II, or by adding on luxury taxes. It puzzles me that socialist planners scarcely mention these possibilities nowadays, and I can only suppose that the folk-memories of the nineteen-forties and early fifties are still vivid enough to overcome the theoretical attractions. In practice this kind of restraint hardly worries the rich and only affects the not-so-rich: inevitably there grows up a black market in pleasure, pursued by a system of penalties and an atmosphere of jealousy and resentment. Authority punishes people for seeking more pleasure than it thinks they ought to have, or for getting more than their 'fair share' of it. Although, as the war showed, it can be enforced it only works for a limited time and if people think it reasonable.

In a consenting democracy persuasion has to precede compulsion: the law sets a seal upon what the majority agrees ought to be done. Today it seems that people are persuaded that it is reasonable to forego the pleasure of using up threatened species in the form of sealskin, osprey feathers, whale oil and ivory. Furs, too, are a great deal less fashionable than they used to be, and these pleasures are foregone not because they are a waste of money but because people are persuaded that they cannot be enjoyed without incurring some intolerable evil. The measurement of 'waste', like the measurement of 'pleasure', is no kind of science at all.

It is an awesome claim (and usually futile) to presume to legislate people into virtuousness without their consent. When governments attempt to, what follows is not really virtue, which involves choice, but at best obedience. I can see few signs that most people – myself included – really believe that the evils of the Consumer Society outweigh its benefits, even if many of its pleasures seem necessary to take away the foul taste of its own making. To return to a hand-made, peasant England might be pleasant enough for a few, but it would condemn the urban working class to drudgery.

I see few signs, either, that most people are persuaded of

the connection between their own relative affluence and the poverty of the Third World. If you were to tell a housewife that she ought not to get a new washing machine because the money is needed for famine relief in Ethiopia, my guess is that she would advise the Ethiopians to stop fighting each other, get a decent government and organise their own affairs better. Being remarkably tender-hearted she would probably put some money in the collecting tin as well; but she would deny that she had any personal responsibility for the impoverishment of Africa, and it would be very hard to prove that she had.

This is not to wash all our hands of the Third World: we should fill every collecting tin to overflowing and struggle to make the world's trading systems more stable. But the housewife would be right in feeling that gestures from afar were not going to affect the systems of power: peoples wish to feed themselves just as they wish to govern themselves, and their greatest enemies in the long run are war and unjust government.

And so, while Ethiopia starves, I sit eating duck in an expensive London restaurant, though by no means every day or even every month. It is an occasional treat to be remembered for a very long time, so I will not spoil it by thinking about loaves and fishes on a Galilean hillside. For all I know, Jesus enjoyed meals almost as good as mine while He dined with His publicans and sinners. Were there, I wonder, beggars at the door?

Nor will I ruin the pleasure by contemplating what I might have done with the time and money spent on my meal. While I try to keep a suspicious eye on my weaknesses I think (without making virtues of them) that I have to reward and refresh them from time to time, like disreputable members of an otherwise respectable crew. After all, they are not such bad fellows. They do not commit too many outrages. They, too, are God's creatures and inseparable members of my complement.

The fact is, between expeditions through its more depressing scenes, I enjoy the pleasures of the world and I find that my conscience (such as it is) will allow me to do so without giving me a moral hangover every morning after. By and large, it is a good and joyful world. There may be some who can celebrate its joy with bread and water, but I fancy they lack the company that I find. I must, of course, be grateful for my pleasures and acknowledge whence they come. I must not mistake those pleasures for the real purpose of life. Nor must I be too selfish about them; for although I may think I have worked hard to earn them, nothing we achieve is done without aid from others, often unseen. Nor, again, must I be envious of those who seem to command even more pleasures than I can. We are often too quick to judge. Who can tell how empty their lives may be, what despair they are trying to drown, what disaster may strike them tomorrow? The last thing Jesus suggests is that the rich are to be envied.

CHAPTER TEN

Blessed are the Poor

Many of my readers and viewers must have emerged from the preceding chapter with the smell of something putrid in their noses. Was not this meant to be about moral standards? Instead of which we had an exercise in casuistry, seeking to ignore the poor on the grounds that Jesus Himself may have enjoyed an occasional good meal.

In fact this book is meant to be about practical moral problems, most of them unresolved; and if I have gained myself little credit, at least I have erred on the side of honesty by making my confession. As I said, life's pleasures offer a moment of relief; but now it is time to do penance.

What can Jesus have meant when He said the poor were blessed? Patently, they were not; and it sounds like pie-in-the-sky Christianity to explain that their blessings awaited them in heaven. Yet this is what St Luke seemed to expect, with his warning to the rich that they had their rewards already. St Matthew seems to have had the humble in mind, with his 'poor in spirit' version. Either way, there was no immediate advantage in the condition; only the assurance that the poor and not the powerful were God's beloved.

And so it must surely be. The message to those of us who are not poor is that we had better get our noses out of our private troughs and serve those who have none to go to, who are sick, homeless, underfed, penniless or put to shame. And it seems to me that Jesus was a good deal less interested in institutional charity than He was in direct personal service by the fortunate to the unfortunate. He would not, I am sure, have decried the work of (say) Christian Aid. But He knew that personally to bind up a leper's sores meant more to both sides than to make a donation to the poor fund and never go near the poor.

But that is the state of most people who will read these pages, and certainly of him who writes them. We are nagged by pressure groups like Shelter, Gingerbread, Age Concern, Child Poverty Action Group, but looking about us we do not readily see the poor and in our daily lives we hardly believe they exist. Surely they are a Dickensian memory made obsolete by the Welfare State; and where they do survive, they must be feckless, incompetent, alcoholic or temporarily unlucky. In some cases, we hear, they actually refuse to work and prefer to sponge off the taxpayer – although remarkably few cases are ever proved, and we are uncomfortably aware that the daily toll of redundancies makes the deliberately idle less and less significant. As I write, there are some three-and-a-half million unemployed in Britain. But the fact that they make little protest (there has not been a riot for over a year) suggests that the dole must be adequate. Poverty, after all, is relative; and relative to thirty, fifty, eighty years ago – let alone in comparison with the employed of India or Nigeria – our unemployed hardly count as poor at all.

But if poverty is relative, relative to what? Should the poor of Victorian London have been content on the grounds that they would have been even worse off in the fourteenth century, or that they were lucky not to be living in Ireland? Or while my children graduate from university, can I rest content that every child in Britain has the chance to get a certificate of secondary education? A nation cannot sit back and call itself prosperous simply on the grounds that, if its wealth were evenly divided, there would be enough for everyone to live comfortably; for the chances are that the wealth is so *un*evenly divided that there are, in effect, two or three nations. The Christian is not merely his brother's keeper, but his neighbour's.

This is not a matter of arguing equal shares for all. There may be a case for that, though I think it is an illusion: what I am arguing is that in our country the minimum income, in cash and services, to avoid falling outside effective society is very much higher than well-to-do people realize and probably beyond the reach of one-fifth to one-quarter of the population.

It is this 'falling outside', exclusion, exile or (to use an ugly piece of jargon) 'marginalization', which is properly seen today as constituting the essence of poverty; for those who have fallen over or been pushed up to the margin are no longer effective members of society. Not only are they deprived of the daily rituals which give order to the lives of the rest of us – the journeying and returning, the working and gathering together; their demand counts for little, they have no way of making their voices heard, and they see themselves having little effect on their surroundings. Thus they become virtually non-persons. To anyone who believes that we all stand equally under the Fatherhood of God, this is deeply sinful. If the world is God's creation and we have been given the stewardship of it, we can have no right to exclude anyone else whom He has seen fit to place here.

Yet we have so elaborated and developed our way of living that there is, in effect, a membership fee to be paid and qualifications presented without which one cannot join in; and such requirements have been rising steadily. It is increasingly hard to make one's mark on society without not only the basic physical necessities like food and housing, but without 'extras' like a car, telephone, information technology, an advanced education, knowledge of how to handle bureaucracy, a good address, an acceptable accent. Even if a 'safety net' is erected so that nobody need starve or be homeless, it is very unlikely to supply the extras. Protestant society, in particular, is opposed to giving people things which it feels they should work for – even when it has made it almost impossible to earn them.

It is only within the last century or so that we have granted that, morally, everyone *ought* to be a full member of society and that the poor should be a thing of the past. As a political reflection of this the vote has been steadily extended until we now have a universal adult franchise, while various kinds of payments have been piled up to ward off destitution. Today they range from retirement and old age pensions to allowances for children and invalids and grants made *ad hoc* to meet necessary bills.

Earlier ages which never imagined that the lower orders had any right to power-sharing saw poverty in strictly material terms. To them, poverty was an act of God and the market, and our ancestors only relieved the poor to prevent their actually dying and to stop them rioting and stealing. For centuries, work was seen as the alternative to disorder, and where poor relief was available it was always made more unpleasant than even the meagre rewards of the lowest forms of labour. The cure for poverty was not to hand out money, but to get the poor back to work no matter how impoverishing the reward. The fact that there were constant bread riots by working people made little impression, for there was a horror of tinkering with the market system which was part of the Law of God. This particular law also happened to be necessary for the success of a labour-intensive factory and farming system.

One cannot altogether brush off the market, for it exists and it is particularly compelling for a nation like Britain which depends so much upon the market of the world. It might be possible to double the wages of underpaid farm-workers and put up the prices of what they produced – but how would you then persuade others not to buy imports without either setting off a trade war or demands for higher wages all round, or both? The market is never so classically perfect as some people pretend – that is one of the fallacies of crude monetarism: the market has always been weighted and distorted and hardly ever responds as the textbooks say it should. But neither can we plan for social justice as if we could opt out of the market altogether. Only an economy which is virtually self-contained and internally regimented can do that and none of the examples that we see today seems to have the wisdom to make a success of it. Once again we return to the sad fact: it is not that nothing can be done, but that less can be done than we would like to do and it takes much longer.

Moral opposition to free handouts for the poor remains influential in Britain. Indeed, there are signs of a return to Victorian standards. But for most of this century the tide has been flowing reluctantly the other way, under the guise of insurance for the disabled and deserving. Unlike the Continent, however, there was prolonged resistance in Britain to the idea of supplementing low wages from public funds, or to any sort of arrangement by state or employer which would give more money to the family man than to the single. In principle this opposition was breached with the post-war family allowances or child benefits and the later family income supplement; but in real terms these have never achieved anything like the importance they hold in France, for example, where a low-paid worker with a large family may get almost as much in family allowances as he earns from his job. This may shock the economic puritan, who will argue that it holds down wages, subsidizes the bad employer and the careless breeder and makes the worker a client of the state. But a legal minimum wage answers part of that; and as for the rest, what is happening is a redistribution of the national wealth at the basic level.

Britain, though, still prefers to keep that base low and to means-test any demands above it. We do not like the idea of public assistance being spent on beer and skittles, or that the poor should have the same right as anyone else to waste what they get, however they may get it. Behind our rules and regulations there seems to lie a grim pleasure in making people suffer for not being like the rest of us; in seeing that they do not enjoy their idleness but are made to realize who is supporting them. We hate to do good for nothing. A no-questions-asked system, like the so-called Negative Income Tax or Tax Credits, would certainly cost more (as indeed more ought to be spent); but means-testing is elaborate and humiliating, and an astonishing number of people either cannot understand it or are repelled by it and fail to get what they are entitled to.

Further failures in aiding the poor are to be seen in our pension and income tax systems. The idea of a progressive income tax is to inflict the least pain on those who can least bear it. But thanks largely to inflation, as well as to the legacy of the war years and the indifference of the well-to-do, the threshold beyond which tax is levied has been persistently too low and the concessions made to the wealthy and the property owner too generous. One result of all this has been the quite unVictorian poverty trap in which it is hardly worth taking a job only to find oneself with less total income than *not* working would yield.

As for retirement pensions, unless an entirely new perspective is established their inadequacy seems to increase with every claim to the contrary. Keeping pace with inflation is nowhere near enough, because society is constantly raising the subscription it demands of people for staying in the game; while, at the same time, retired people are living longer, increasing in numbers, and needing more facilities for survival.

In fact the position of the retired has always held the seeds of catastrophe and it is remarkable that they have been resigned to it so long. From what was probably their maximum earning power they slip overnight to half that, at best, and often to a great deal less. The most competent, who usually include the highest earners and those who have never been unemployed, will have made provision against this and have little to complain about. But far too many either struggle to stay on in the homes to which they justly feel entitled, or else uproot themselves and go to live in reduced circumstances among strangers. Attempts to create a special economy-class Old Age Pensioners' community only emphasize the fact that retired people are being pushed out of society to join the ranks of the ineffectual.

Why should people have to retire if they do not want to? Ideally, they should not. But there are at least two forces pressing them to do so: the ambition of the younger people below them, tired of waiting for the log-jam to break, and the pressure to make vacancies at a time of unemployment. Both are short-sighted, but together they make it difficult to install a policy of voluntary, open-ended retirement. Even a policy of demoting people towards the end of their careers and adjusting their pay so as to provide a higher pension closer to their final earnings would have serious difficulties: many people would resent being cut back in their prime and would rather get the maximum salary while they were working than gamble on living to enjoy a higher pension. However we look at it it seems to me that there will eventually be no alternative to taxing off a higher proportion of the wages of those who are working and redistributing it to those who are not. We can only hope that the employed greatly outnumber the unemployed and that they are as productive as possible, for it will make no sense to create jobs that make losses.

I have already expressed surprise that the elderly, the unemployed and the low-paid – now the three largest groups outside effective society – do not make us more aware of their predicament. There are, of course, other groups overlapping them like single-parent families, black people, the physically and mentally handicapped, the homeless and down-and-out. It may be argued that they are less badly off than I have suggested: after all, most of them get at least the minimum diet and manage to survive the winter, and I myself seem to be dodging the issue of whether they are actually destitute. Surely if they were they would have let us know in no uncertain way. But even the periodic 'marches for jobs' seem to lack suffering; and we know they are organized by those very trade unions whose exorbitant demands (according to the market economists) priced the marchers out of their jobs.

We come to the unions in a later chapter. In the meantime, there are several factors it is easy for us to overlook: first of all, that the poor are bad at protesting and the well-to-do are bad at seeing poverty. Almost by definition, the well-to-do do not live in poor areas and do not mix with the poor. Despite attempts by sociologically-minded journalists (which are not popular with media bent upon entertainment), the middle classes are remarkably ill-informed about what it is like to lose one's job and try to maintain a home and family on the dole and its various supplements. Most of us have or know of unemployed middle-class children or pensioner relatives. We do not easily empathize with what life is like for them, but the chances are that it is cushioned by the family and that middle-class know-how will triumph in the end. It is highly unlikely that many readers will have any experience of whole families and neighbourhoods unplugged from society and left to rot. The poor, who share neither our activities nor our language, have almost no way of telling us.

To begin with they are often winded by what has happened to them and ashamed of themselves for letting it happen. People who have managed to support themselves in the past, even if they are really victims of the economic system, instinctively feel their predicament must be their own fault. Free-loaders do exist: I heard of one young man who made a comfortable living by fathering children on unmarried girls (an achievement for which he enjoyed a high reputation in the neighbourhood) and then collecting a percentage of their weekly benefit, to the satisfaction of all concerned. But most people are remarkably conscientious and eager to assume responsibility for their own maintenance: when they have to accept public assistance to tide them over, they are grateful for it. They begin by seeing themselves as they once saw others and do not want to be thought whingers or spongers. The very idea of making a spectacle of themselves by parading through the streets and shouting at cabinet ministers is abhorrent to them; it would draw attention to their personal failure.

People whose morale has been undermined by disaster do not usually have the spirit to make a fuss; and because they hope that their troubles are temporary – that they will soon be back at work – are hard to organize in any way that seems to brand them with a new identity as 'one of the unemployed' or 'one of the poor'. And so the rest of us do not hear them, do not understand them and are not much moved to do something about them. Looking back down the early nineteen-eighties it seems to me there was a feeling, even among the unemployed themselves, that the nation had had it too good and was being justly punished for its over-ambition.

A different trap catches many of those whose poverty is long-term or permanent: they get used to it and learn to cope. Particularly if their background is one of low expectations they devise a kind of sub-life, shared with others, so that an impoverished neighbourhood develops its own solidarity, even its own wit and gaiety. You see this taken to the extreme in a country like India, where whole colonies of untouchables accept the most outrageous discrimination and still manage to celebrate their weddings and festivals with gusto. Britain, too, has its caste system and its underclasses which accept that certain things are 'not for the likes of us'. This attitude is fading steadily under the enticements of the advertisers and their supermarkets, but perhaps the well-to-do should be grateful it has endured so long.

Grateful, too, that so many people do not realize they are poor and living below the official poverty-line: something like seven million people at the time of writing. If they do not realize it, it might be argued that they should not be counted as poor; but that is rather like being ill without realizing it. It is also like saying that if people do not demand their rights, others need feel no duty towards them. The Christian should know very well that when he possesses more than he needs he has a positive duty to use it for the service of those whom he can see to be needy, without being asked. And 'need' he must now define not just in terms of food, roof and clothing but of everything that is required to help his neighbour join in the society and make his own contribution to it.

If Christians take the Bible at all seriously, they must see it in terms of God trying to lead *the entire community of His people* forward, with the privileged caring for the underprivileged and not merely saving their own souls. And if God seeks to liberate His people from bondage and exalt the humble and meek, then those who (like Moses) are privileged have to awaken His people to the injustice of their position – awakening also the consciences of those who are failing in their duty by not changing that position – and lead the exiles to the Promised Land which they could have, because it is there for them and not just for the powerful. This, I think, is not Marxism but Judaeo-Christianity.

The Promised Land, we know, was not easily come by. The one in the Bible was, unfortunately, stolen from its occupiers, and periodically lost or spoilt. It is no good assuming that ours is waiting ready for us, flowing with milk and honey, to be divided up. In fact it will never be perfected, any more than the Children of Israel's was; but that will not be accepted as an excuse for abandoning the long march, or for whoring after strange gods on the way.

During the election campaign of May 1983, all the political parties promised more jobs; but all of them admitted it would take time. In a letter to the main party leaders, the chairman of Church Action on Poverty, the Reverend John Austin, wrote: 'What is needed is immediate help for the poor, to stop the disintegration of our society into two nations.' And he went on to outline the dimensions of the crisis: 'The number of those living on Supplementary Benefit has risen from four to seven million over the last three years . . . The total number of those living on or below that level is approaching the ten million mark if it has not already passed it.'

The poverty that really exists in Britain today can be seen in three overlapping ways. First, there are those who are visibly and obviously destitute, the problem cases on the books of the social services or charity workers. Second, there is the poverty of those whose suffering is not so obvious, who manage to tick over on low wages or state assistance but have nothing left over with which to participate actively in society. And third, affecting us all as a nation, but especially these two groups, there are whole areas of 'structural poverty' where important parts of the social and economic systems have become worn out and neglected. There is something to be said for the theory that things will not really improve until those systems are replaced, but readers of my chapters on politics and business will recall how reluctant I am to put my trust in the perfectibility of systems. In the here and now we cannot be forgiven for overlooking what is often sneered at as 'reformism', for it offers the best hope of rescuing people who are actually on our doorstep.

Governments tinker endlessly with various ways of maintaining what we might call the upper poor, or disadvantaged, offering them pensions, unemployment pay, supplementary benefits, disability allowances, family income supplements and child benefits according to circumstances. It might seem obvious to organize the whole system as a gigantic insurance policy paid for by members' contributions, and there has always been an element of this. But the approach breaks down on the national scale, because what the disadvantaged can afford to pay in will never be able to finance what they will eventually need to draw out; and with such vast sums involved, no government can keep the benefit funds and the general revenue separated. Nor has anyone been able to forecast what inflation, fate and politics would demand in the years ahead. Social justice is a developing concept. We cannot tell the disadvantaged that their income must be limited to what their past contributions have earned them (in some cases, nothing): we have to start redistributing what society is earning now.

In addition to the fact that society may not seem to be earning enough – the upper poor of today would be even worse off without the unearned income of the North Sea – attempts to redistribute have to overcome a variety of resentments: the resentment of those who have actually got the money and see little justice in surrendering it to those who had nothing to do with it; the resentment of those who suspect they are being asked to help undermine the rules of a game they are winning; and the resentment of those who feel themselves virtuous towards those who are apparently negligent. Much of this resentment might dissolve if the well-to-do were more accustomed to dealing justly with each other; but people who suspect they are not getting a fair deal among themselves are not likely to grant it to people below them. They are unmoved by arguments that money is more effectively spent by the poor, or that low pay leads to inefficient industry, yet there is reason to believe that both these arguments are true. The greatest single cause of poverty is, quite simply, that people are not being paid enough. This may well be because they are badly utilized by their employers, but I am persuaded that a national minimum wage – perhaps about two-thirds the average male earnings – would be the biggest single contribution that could be made towards breaking the problem.

A society which harbours such resentments and ignores

these arguments is ill-equipped to deal with the lower poor, those who are visibly down and out. It is handicapped, also, by the legacy of the 'sixties based upon the conviction that any competent individual could look forward to a steadily rising standard of life and that it did not much matter if private affluence was accompanied by public squalor. The fact that the number of unfortunates turning to the Welfare State was growing steadily tended to be explained in terms of lack of competence, almost as if it were a mental illness and therefore to be 'treated' on an individual or family basis. What such people needed, it was argued, was a better environment or training in how to cope. Undoubtedly there were, and are, families that could not cope, particularly with the shortage of cash; but many of them could not cope, either, with the bureaucratic complications of the Welfare State and the economic system of which it was part.

The causes of lower poverty have always been the same, and those who have analysed them in Britain have never rated reluctance to work as important among them. The death or sickness of the breadwinner, loss of work, low pay, and the arrival of children are the outstanding causes; though the kind of family which is accused of breeding recklessly is usually in trouble from the start. One survey of poor families in Nottingham (1970)[1] found that one-fifth of the one-child families, one-third of the two-child families and almost half of the three-child families surveyed were in poverty. For many working people there has been, for generations, a pattern of crossing and re-crossing the line: poverty in childhood, relative affluence as they went out to work and got married, poverty with the arrival of children, renewed affluence as the teenagers brought home money, and poverty again as they left the parents to retirement and old age.

The state has done something to blunt the more savage of these blows; but it has never sought to maintain the worker

[1] *Poverty – The Forgotten Englishmen*, Coates & Silburn; Pelican

in the position he may have reached, so that he can carry on upwards when he has recovered. He may only have reached that position by working long hours of overtime or by sending his wife out to work as well, and at a time of widespread unemployment neither of these may be available again. Meanwhile, in working society the standards of living continue to rise, and the gap between those who have stayed in the game and those who have been counted out of it widens. The 'shaking out' of the labour force which has been going on, with higher productivity being secured from those who have kept their jobs, makes it very unlikely that re-employment will restore as many as half the jobless to the living standards of their working contemporaries.

The reliance of so many families upon *two* adult wages – the husband's and the wife's – puts these families, also, in danger. Loss of work by either partner, divorce, desertion or pregnancy can devastate them. And although our society seems to have removed the stigma from the one-parent family, it has still not made up its mind whether it should merely keep it alive or positively bring it up (and if so, how).

One of the cruellest traps into which our poor have fallen is that the great majority of them have to live in the worst possible places to be poor in: decayed industrial areas and inner cities. It was employment that brought them there and paid for their social wage as well as their cash income, but where employment has collapsed there is neither pay for the ex-workers nor rates to maintain their environment. They may be lucky enough to be housed in new, or new-ish council estates: but how lucky is that, in fact? Much of our post-war housing has proved inhuman and hostile to its inhabitants: whole acreages are shunned as if they were cursed. Communications are often bad, shops distant and fuel costs high, and the genuine spirit of community non-existent. The poor may get their rent and rates paid for them, but then comes the trap of losing those subsidies if earned income rises too high; and 'difficult cases' get shunted into a council's less desirable properties.

The problem of those who are unavoidably homeless, who do not qualify for respectable housing under any approved category and can no longer afford temporary accommodation at their own expense, is getting more serious with every month that passes. The wandering dosser, the meths drinker, dropout or drug addict whose traditional refuge was the charitable hostel, has been joined by increasing numbers of young unemployed.

But surely, if slowly, the Recession will recede and the sun will shine again in these dark corners? I have read no economist or politician who has dared to prophesy that things will ever be as they were twenty years ago, and I fear, myself, they may get far worse than they are now. Then we shall become more aware of that third level of poverty which has bitten so deep: the poverty which has infected so many of the structures and systems which we have taken for granted – the roads, railways, drains, factories, public buildings as well as housing. In the North of England, Scotland, Northern Ireland and Wales in particular, whole regions not merely have their poor people – they *are* poor. They even vote a kind of poverty politics which has little hope of being taken into account by the affluent power systems of the South. There is a real danger of their becoming demoralized, discredited and self-destructive.

Industrially, such areas face the danger of being written off as untouchable, a bad address for anyone in search of a home for a new industry. Who would want to go to a town where the very walls speak of failure?

Over us looms the shadow of a visibly two-nation Britain: half of it having survived into recovery and pulling further and further ahead; the other half – the under-classes – stuck in subsidized poverty and kept there by those very services which should have been easing the way out. I think not only of the urban amenities, nor of the tax and welfare systems, but of one particular service which has betrayed the people – I mean our public education system. This is not the fault of the teachers, who are as much its victims as their pupils, and it is not to be solved at a stroke by abolishing the fee-paying schools and turning Eton into a comprehensive.

A bee in my bonnet this may be, but I think we should smart from its sting. Compared with the Continent and North America, Britain's well-to-do have little respect for education among their own ranks: for the working classes they seem to view it as a way to keep children off the streets until it is time for them to start moving crates or filling boxes. In a world which is becoming more and more sophisticated and dependent upon the handling of information, we cut down our educational resources and treat our schools and universities with contempt. The children of the under-classes sense this, and it is hardly surprising that they find no connection between the time they serve in the class-room and the jobless world outside. When jobs are advertised, too many of them cannot even read what is wanted or write their application in response.

Our coal mines may all shut down and our blast furnaces turn cold, but the British could still make a living with their brains: they could write, design, perform, research, teach, bank, trade, insure *and* farm or manufacture – provided they took their children's educaton seriously and regarded it as something that we never, in fact, complete. As it is, we bury our talents, hide our lights under bushels and offend greatly against our little ones. Britain's poor are condemned to poverty in the class-room. The well-to-do must pay for their discharge, as they must for a great deal else.

CHAPTER ELEVEN

Work or What?

The birthplace of the Industrial Revolution lies today in ruins as tranquil as Verulamium or Old Sarum. Coalbrookdale, where in 1709 Abraham Darby, the Quaker, first smelted iron with coke instead of charcoal, and Ironbridge, where his grandson Abraham Darby III erected the first iron bridge across the Severn, are now an award-winning display of industrial archaeology; and to complete the irony the Shropshire New Town of Telford, which they both adjoin, has a higher rate of unemployment than Northern Ireland and has been declared an Enterprise Zone in the hopes of attracting back some enterprise.

Like the ruined tin mines of Cornwall, the antique furnaces and blowing engines have acquired a certain picturesqueness – though in its heyday the Gorge must have looked like the mouth of hell. More depressing now is the decay all over Britain of work itself as we had come to expect it. During the election campaign of 1983, the cry from Labour was for jobs, jobs, jobs: yet it had remarkably little impact upon the voters because (I seemed to detect) there was a guilty feeling that the nation was being justly punished for its hubris, that it had brought unemployment upon itself by its past excesses, and that – for all the promises of socialist planning – things could never be the same again. What I want to discuss now is not so much who was to blame as what the moral implications are of this collapse of the *inevitability* of work. Must we work at all costs, and what becomes of us if we cannot?

I have said before that I am reluctant to accept even the most confident predictions of the future. For all I know, twenty years from now, Britain may be wallowing in undreamed of prosperity, though it seems unlikely. Farmers and businessmen that I have talked to invariably told me that if the economy turned upwards they would be happy to increase their output, but not by employing more people if they could help it. Employees had proved far more trouble than they were worth and they had indeed 'priced themselves out of a job'. One small country businessman who had halved his workforce in three years told me: 'It's no good saying I don't care for my crew when it's all I can do to keep the ship afloat. I've got my competitors, my bank manager, my taxman and the union on my heels – keeping them at bay just doesn't leave me anything to play Father Christmas with.' And so he had paid off the old men early, stopped taking apprentices, and bought some new machinery. His chief worry was that his products might be getting out of date and he had nothing to spare for research and development. Most of this he blamed on excessive pay increases given in the 1970s as an easy way out, though I think, myself, that the trouble was much older and more complicated.

The guilty silence of the unemployment issue in 1983 was the silence not just of people who felt they had brought their troubles upon themselves – many would have denied that – but also of those who were still comfortably off and did not want to draw too much attention to it. It reflected the two nations: one unemployed and powerless – the other still employed and anxious not to risk the basis of their power. There is more to this than money, though the money that comes (with few exceptions) only to the employed is very important. The fact is that in our society unless you can say *what* you are – which means what you do – you are not accepted as an effective participant in the game of life.

To be able to say 'I am a steel-worker – a bank manager –

a journalist' registers on two levels. It establishes you as competent and self-supporting, to be taken seriously as an autonomous human being and not (however unfairly) as a failure. And the British class system being as it is, it also establishes you in a hierarchy of power and influence. Bank managers, I find, are usually treated more deferentially than either journalists or steel-workers. It is true that the unemployed still have the vote, but voting does not happen very often and the man or woman who loses a job feels that he or she no longer has any power to affect the life of the community, that he or she is no longer needed, and suffers a loss of self-esteem which may be very much worse than the loss of esteem from others. In Christian terms this ought not to be so: it is not *what* a person is but *how* a person is that matters: but the eyes of the world are looking for other signs.

Our jobs, even more than our clothes, our homes and our friends, are powerful ways of expressing the sort of people we are. They have a profound moral value, for they say something about our view of the purpose of living; and a morally good society will allow its citizens the fullest opportunity to choose a job which seems to them worth doing. It is, of course, not quite as simple as that: there are handicaps and privileges in the way; even without them, supply may exceed demand and talents fail to match aspirations. I myself would sooner have been a musician than anything else, but am simply not good enough.

But when people are forced into occupations which are meaningless to them, or are denied any active role at all, then they are being deprived of a choice which would help to define their identity and make them effective people. I would say such a society had failed in its duty to them. Mass unemployment is wrong not because it gives people less money than they would like and deprives the trade union movement of membership fees, but because for most people work is the most important framework within which they can make their moral assertions. If there are few such opportunities in many production jobs, then that is an indication of how work itself has become dangerously inhuman. Our work should be a way of searching for and expressing God's vision of our true nature, and of developing those talents with which He has entrusted each one of us. It must be sinful to exclude human beings from such an opportunity, though that leaves open the possibility that they may have excluded themselves.

This notion of work – of creative engagement with the material world and other people – as a form of spiritual growth is not, perhaps, the commonest Christian approach. Despite the Carpenter of Nazareth, the fishermen apostles and tent-making St Paul, the early Church drifted towards the view that the holiest of men ought to withdraw from the world and as soon engage in labour or commerce as they would in marriage. God's sentence upon Adam – 'In the sweat of thy brow shalt thou eat bread . . .' – seemed to identify work as a punishment rather than a duty. It is true that, through the Middle Ages, the Church was happy to endorse the feudal view of peasant servitude (and I have already said enough about work as an instrument of law and order), but such holidays as there were came from the Church and were drastically cut down after the Reformation.

The Protestant reformers read their Bibles differently. God had given Adam dominion over the earth and its resources. He had renewed that covenant with Noah. Man was God's steward upon earth and must not be an idle one. The talents entrusted to Man must be made to yield the utmost possible. There were plenty of indications (in the Old Testament, at any rate) that he whom the Lord loved prospered, so there was no reason to be ashamed of the profits, provided one praised God for them and obeyed His commandments. It was all too easy to overlook Jesus's extension of these to include priority for the poor; indeed, by the eighteenth century it was being argued that the poor were only suffering the divinely ordained consequences of not trying hard enough.

But this was a peversion of the original Protestantism – if so we may describe the teachings of John Ball and Wycliffe; and it was never the view of Calvin, either. He believed that the sharing of earthly goods with one's neighbour was mandatory, and he refused to have labour treated as a mere commodity in the market. Martin Luther, who, as we know, was no admirer of ecclesiastical pretentions, endowed secular dedication with as much dignity as religious vocation: both were offerings in service to God, and in the world a man had the daily duty to extend charity to his fellows. Both Luther and Calvin saw hard work as a Christian obligation and there is little doubt that in doing so they helped prepare the ground for capitalism and industrial economy. There were occasional complaints about the corrupting effect upon society of spreading the wealth – religion and riches have seldom gone well together – but there were examples like the Quaker ironmasters of Coalbrookdale to suggest that prosperity and morality *could* go hand-in-hand.

So we arrive at the 'Protestant work ethic', still advocated by evangelical industrialists like Sir Fred Catherwood, writing[1]: 'The Christian does not work to earn a living; he works because God intended that he should use the gifts He had given him for the fulfilment of a divine purpose. He goes on working whether or not he needs to earn a living. His work is a divine vocation and not to be treated lightly . . . No labour is degrading.'

Catherwood, though, insists upon the highest degree of personal responsibility for the job and what we make of it. It is not just hard work but 'intellectual integrity' that he demands, and by this he means that we should 'be much more conscious than others of our standards of service . . .

[1] *The Christian in Industrial Society*, Catherwood; Inter-Varsity Press

Too often the Christian is no better than the next man.' And the writer goes on to deplore the visible decline of the Protestant work ethic: 'All the talk is of shorter working hours and greater leisure.' British workers have slowed down in order to keep their jobs, while the more easily collectivised Orientals have run away with western methods of mass production. To respond by intensifying collectivisation in the West is to impose almost intolerable burdens upon the Christian who cannot unload his personal responsibility upon the collective, be it union or company. Advocating smaller plants and team production, Catherwood concludes that a Christian society has to find new ways of creating and distributing wealth.

In short, things have become too big because the logic of the system has not been challenged by the individual conscience. We have failed to assert our power to question its morality and to impose our human choices on it. But, in a sense, we have made ourselves the victims of the Protestant ethic which Catherwood so much admires. To do him justice, he is most anxious that the Christian worker should select his vocation with care, asking himself constantly what he is doing and why. But very few of us have the chance to be so choosy. Industry is based upon the worker accepting a duty to make more than he needs for his own living: that is the consequence of the Protestant ethic as Catherwood states it, and it also happens to be the essence of the capitalist system. But it only becomes technically possible by managers organising production in ways which constantly remove the right of choice from the individual – just as the most effective way to resist the system is for organised labour to do the same. The system may be interpreted or justified as embodying a divine vocation or as maximising profits, but so far as the masses are concerned it comes down to the pursuit of work for its own sake and almost without question.

The election cry for 'Jobs, jobs, jobs!' never presses on to say what kind of jobs. It seems that any jobs will do. We seldom ask ourselves whether we need to work so hard (the British, typically, have longer hours, fewer holidays and later retirement than anyone else in Europe), or whether our product is necessary, desirable or over-priced. We just work; and I suspect that many of us do so primarily because we enjoy the human relationships involved and the shape that working gives to our lives.

But I have ignored one perfectly obvious reason for work – that it earns our living; and there are good biblical grounds for insisting that 'if any would not work, neither should he eat'. At the back of my mind there lies a suspicion that the link between the two has been established to satisfy the ambitions of the powerful rather than the necessities of the workers, nevertheless it seems only natural justice that idlers should not be allowed to live as parasites of the industrious – and even more obvious that if nobody is making anything there will be nothing for anybody.

However, things become less straightforward as the exceptions present themselves. It is totally unbiblical to allow the unproductive sick, the elderly and the handicapped to starve, and, as we have seen, our society can no longer countenance the grossest disparities between rich and poor. It redistributes at least a portion of the riches to those who have not strictly earned them and who may not even be working at all. Would anyone say it was actually sinful to pay an allowance to an eighteen-year-old West Indian unmarried mother in Dalston? Perhaps they would. But it seems to me that such payments, like the dole to the unemployed, reflect the judgment of society that deprivation diminishes us all, regardless of desert, and that most of today's poor are not to blame for their condition. We are not, even in the present neo-Victorian climate, going to return to the Poor Law of 1834.

What we are tending to do – very imperfectly – is to average out the community's income, just as a family might, and to pay less attention to personal merit. Whether you see this as a dangerously unprotestant sign of collectivisation or as a truly Christian recognition that we are all members one of another is, perhaps, a matter of taste. But neither answers the problem of how a sharing, caring society is actually going to make any wealth to share if it devotes more care to morality than productivity.

It might be highly moral to break up our industries into small workshops, refusing to use any but recycled materials or to make unnecessary gadgets or weapons of war. But would this not hand over even more of our markets, at home and abroad, to our competitors and leave all of us, including the poor, more impoverished?

It is all very well to denounce the inhumanities of mass production; but it is human beings who buy its output, spend its wages and enjoy its benefits, and with considerable enthusiasm. We are forced to come to terms with the industrial market system by the fact that it is a worldwide system and we are part of the world, not isolated from it. Britain might be able to devise a system which was in theory more just and humane *if* she were able to cut herself off from competition and trade. But it would not be sustainable, and from a Christian point of view I would argue that it was morally wrong. It is not only a matter of reducing choices. If we are called upon to share with our neighbour in the care and enjoyment of God's creation, we cannot be selfishly nationalistic about it.

It may be argued that Britain's present system is not sustainable, either; but in a crippled fashion, it is. What we are seeing now is less employment producing less output and a lower average income per head (taking unemployed with employed). Work goes on, as it must if we are to have any imports or income at all, and people have adapted to the situation far better than those in power have had any right to expect. It seems that what we have to contemplate next is one of two things: either a further decline all round, or an

increase in both employment and output which will nevertheless still leave large numbers of people without work but
almost certainly demanding a bigger share of the earnings
of those who *have* jobs. Whichever happens, we will have to
rethink the relationship between work and income, and that
means the whole Protestant work ethic. If two to four
million people – and perhaps even more – are to be per-
manently on the dole, what becomes of that duty to work
hard and conscientiously as a service to God through their
fellow men? What are they to *do* in order to establish their
identity, self-respect and meaningfulness? How are they to
avoid becoming second class citizens observing lower
standards of behaviour? And how is it to be determined
what share of the national income they are to receive?

It is tempting to say that the unemployed could find work
if only they would accept lower wages and tighter discipline. But we have already seen the poverty-trap of low
wages, which do nothing to lift the poor into effective
society, while the sort of work which attracts low pay is
seldom the sort to inspire discipline or respect. In any case
unskilled labour is precisely the sort which gets replaced by
labour-saving machinery, and we have to face the fact that
what has been going on is not only a trade recession but a
new industrial revolution brought on by the robot and the
microchip. To take only one early example, hundreds of
thousands of laundry jobs were destroyed by the arrival of
the laundrette and the domestic washing-machine, and
although some were gained in the manufacture of the
equipment many of them were lost again when manufacture was automated or went abroad. There are those who
argue that alternative jobs can be opened up in the new
technologies, but these tend to be extremely economical in
their use of manpower, and the type of employees they
require are usually of a higher grade than those who have
been displaced lower down the system. I guess there are
very few ex-laundry workers making washing machines

today, let alone writing computer software or controlling airline traffic. We are back in the British education trap, and since this is unlikely to be demolished in the near future by a stroke of anyone's pen, we must struggle grimly with things as they are rather than as they ought to be.

A certain amount of tinkering can be done. Some jobs, though not all, can be shared by those who can afford to work part-time; but the experiments already conducted found few takers. The benefits of early retirement are even more debatable. Can firms afford to finance it? Will people stand for reduced pensions? Can they be forced to stop working if they do not want to? Sabbaticals, in-job training, educational leave, all sound attractive, but they assume that employers (or the state) have the money to spare for non-productive employees. An agency system under which a person's career would be 'managed' through a pattern of alternating appointments and educational periods has been suggested, but it would probably only make sense for high flyers.

Most drastic of all is the proposal that nobody should be entitled by law to more than a certain ration of years at work, and that for the remainder they should receive a payment from the state based upon age, qualifications, family needs and other variables. At first sight this has the appeal of fairness, but I cannot help feeling it would be political dynamite to handle, there would surely have to be numerous exemptions, besides a grave temptation to moonlight and evade.

If we ever did arrive at a situation where half the population was in skilled, well-paid employment while the other half was maintained at subsistence level, we could find ourselves slipping into a kind of mediaeval attitude of the well-to-do patronizing the poor with menial tasks, public entertainments and charity. It would not be an ennobling situation, and certainly not one for which the Labour Movement has prepared the hitherto-working classes. We could easily find ourselves with a deprived and mutinous urban peasantry seen as such a threat to the middle classes and their property that they had to be firmly repressed by the forces of law and order. Identity cards, curfews, political offences, detention camps, the penal use of Social Security, even executions, are not mere bogeys of the imagination: they are the only ways such a system has been dealt with in the past, and in the future the backlash from them would be as terrible as the repression itself. It seems to me one of the strongest moral reasons why we must not allow such a division between working and non-working to take root in our country. The old suspicion that people would riot if they were not kept at work was usually exaggerated; but the difference today is that revolutionary terrorism and counter-revolutionary repression have become highly developed systems in themselves, liable to start feeding off each other even though neither was morally justified.

This is an essay in ethics rather than a treatise on politics and economics, and admittedly it is much easier to condemn evils than to cure them. Even if we could analyse our problems objectively, we are neither wise enough to understand all their causes nor powerful enough to manipulate them. Undoubtedly we are suffering from a world-wide disease and we cannot (perhaps should not) opt out of it. That is not to say our own domestic policies have been entirely blameless: I think the 1983 elections showed that we know this and, with some wisdom, do not expect any remedies to take effect more speedily than the causes did. But one of the saddest events of the election year was the aimless and ill-prepared Williamsburg Summit Conference which revealed no will on any country's part to surrender sovereignty in the interests of the general good – perhaps hardly surprising, when every statesman there must have known that his own people were not prepared to make such a surrender.

So we have to start – as experts like the Brandt Commission and the relief and development agencies have been telling us for years – by accepting our interdependence with the developing nations and our ability to make sacrifices for them. That is what has been lacking over the past forty years of relations between the First World and Second World and the Third (and between rich and poor generally): the redemptive element of sacrifice by the well-to-do. Notably, debts have to be forgiven. We have to shoulder the burden of turning what were envisaged as loans into gifts. This may be bad banking – the loans would have to be spread among the donor nations and their tax-payers, also – but it would be far less damaging than the collapse of the borrowers, and it would also be immaculately biblical. We might then hope that, relieved of debt, the developing nations would become better trading partners and generators of employment in our own exporting industries. 'Trade, not aid' is what the developing world aspires to, and once we have wiped the slate clean we can face each other in dignity and equality.

By itself this will not achieve miracles. I do not think there will be any miracles, certainly not any sudden return to full employment (which we will probably never see again). The making of artificial jobs which do not earn more than their own keep is illusory and insulting: it will not fool those who get such jobs that they are really needed by society, and a manager would be justified in regarding such draftees as a handicap and a potential source of trouble.

Trouble with labour in the form of strikes, restrictive practices and excessive wage demands is a fruitful field for moralizing. It points, of course, to *the unions*, and while few pretend that there would actually be more jobs without the unions unemployment has helped to provide the opportunity for cutting them down to size. It is probably worth reminding ourselves what the justifications are for their intervention in the world of work.

By definition, management is in a commanding position over employment. Unless restricted by law, management has the power to hire and fire, it has the workplace and the machinery, the raw materials and distribution network and, above all, it has the money. In comparison, the worker has nothing but his muscles and his skill, and unless these are exceptional there will be far more alternatives to him than there will be to a potential employer. As industry has developed, more and more employers have become established in positions of virtual monopoly, so that an employee would find himself obliged to accept whatever pay and conditions the management chose to offer, since to refuse would mean no work and no pay. Untampered with, their relative powers would be those of an elephant and a mouse. But for the past century and more there has been considerable tampering.

The only way an employee can achieve anything like equal strength is by building up a similar monopoly position. So he bands together with his fellow workers as one man, and informs the employer that unless pay and conditions are satisfactory there will be no labour at all and so no production, no sales, no income for the company. The union has been saving up for just such a rainy day and is prepared to sit out the siege.

Usually there are negotiations involving what the workers say they need to live and how their pay compares with other workers, what the management says it can afford and what its competitors are doing. Usually a good deal of threatening and bluffing is involved, but usually a compromise is reached. Few managements are as grinding today as they undoubtedly were in the past, but most workers are convinced their pay would have been far worse without union pressure. Managements prefer – or say they prefer – to work with a union and one seldom hears about the great minority of cases in which there is no disruption of work. The Quaker Darbys were scarcely bothered by unions, but they were always known as just and generous employers, and I am persuaded that even today as much of our trouble is due to inadequate management as to militant unionism. Whatever the causes – historical, political, social, educational or sheer exhaustion – there seems to have been a failure of national character to supply the kind of leadership required for modern industry. It is almost as if we were no longer interested in making and selling things well. Abraham Darby II positively enjoyed investing and expanding, and seemed to regard it as quite secondary that there might be something over for his own pocket.

What has seldom happened in British industry is for labour and management to grow together and regard the enterprise as their joint responsibility. The existence of an absentee third party – the shareholders – has something to do with this. But even more important is the inertia of history and the impersonal logic of a system which seeks productive efficiency with too little regard to the way of life it is creating for those engaged in it. When the assembly-line workers at British Leyland's Cowley plant went on strike rather than give up a few minutes' 'washing-up time', they were not being bloody-minded. They were resisting the last straw that was breaking them down into machines, and they felt that those who were giving the orders had no idea what life was like for them. Faced with impersonal and unreasoning management which had given them too few opportunities for choice, the workers took refuge in an impersonal and unreasoning trade union structure.

Clearly industry cannot be run purely for the benefit of the workers – any more than it should be purely for the benefit of the balance sheet. When a moral choice is admitted, there has to be some sort of compromise between the two involving the reflections of conscience; and conscience, as the Church insists, has to be informed. One of the things which ought to inform it, for it is central to the Christian attitude to work, is a sense of service and duty –

unfashionable virtues, and suspect to militant unionists on the grounds that they are mere disguises for capitalist domination. But a Christian worker does have a duty to serve – as does a Christian manager. Nor is that duty only towards one another. It is, above all, towards the community for which they are supposed to be providing goods and services, and which ultimately pays them. It cannot possibly be right for the two sides of an industry to ignore their duty to the community and wage their disputes as if there were no one else involved.

Some disputes go far beyond argument: they break out into strikes, 'blacking' and picketing. When fundamental public services like coal, water, electricity, transport and hospitals are concerned, this is bound to bring inconvenience and even suffering to the very people who have every reason to expect the service. This again cannot be morally right. What, however, are workers to do who believe there is no other way of obliging management to take their grievances seriously? If management has the ultimate weapon of paying or not paying, surely the union must have the equivalent weapon of working or not working – though, to be sure, its members expect to get their jobs back and do not seriously mean to resign them or put the inadequacy of their pay to the proof by challenging anyone else to do the work. Unions, indeed, would be outraged if managements turned the tables and fought back tit for tat. What we have now is a one-sided use of total warfare, complete with indifference towards the innocent civilian casualty. Now that large parts of industry and many big unions are ruled by political guide-lines, the warfare is on an increasing scale.

If people cannot be persuaded that Christian principles of service and sacrifice must take precedence in industry (and there are few signs of that happening in the near future) the only alternative to warfare, as in inter-personal and international relations, must be binding contract and judgment according to law. This has been strenuously resisted in Britain, because the law has been seen as politically biased (as it is likely to be under the British electoral system): but the time has surely come when disputes must be made justiciable, if only to protect employment itself.

The threat that it will not work because it will be made unworkable is one that no moral person can afford to yield to. Over the years the language of industrial relations has been dangerously undermined. Too often neither side understands what the other is talking about, because each has different objectives or a different mythological image of what it stands for. Labour does not see itself as an equal partner in industry, with equal dignity: it is still the revolting peasantry, exploited by the bosses. Workers are concerned with maintaining a tolerable way of life *in spite of* the work they have to do; while management is concerned with advancing production in spite of the preferences of the workers. There is so little opportunity left for choice, that relations have become a struggle between two systems, regardless of any moral considerations that might be over and above both. There is little common ground between them because the actual making of the product has become something apart from the fulfilment of those making it. Paradoxically, even the fact that the product earns them their pay is no longer enough to keep men working.

And so the union is obliged to show itself as formidable in its own way as the company it confronts, and its full-time officials become personifications of that toughness, speaking the language of intransigence. Whatever the rights and wrongs in moral terms, the union is forced to follow the laws of solidarity, militancy and inflexibility, while the company is driven on by the market. Trapped in these systems, identified as the sort of people who are utterly loyal to them and deprived of choice, negotiators find it hard to resort to any common language which might allow them to admit to weaknesses or doubts.

I suspect that insofar as we are going to find a solution to the problems of work, the seeds have already been sown. There will be some, inadequate, revival of business. Government will resort to Keynesian stimulation on a cautious scale, and union members will slowly tiptoe away from their more strident leaders. A surprising number of people are already adapting themselves to a simpler, occasionally-employed way of life, and many others are setting up profitably in small personal enterprises. Families are having to support each other much longer and provide their own work by doing things for themselves, and I fancy we will learn to spread such wealth as there is by inventing little, useful jobs about the community. Our future living will be more precarious, more adventurous, perhaps, and less wasteful. It could be made easier by a less bureaucratic view of how life ought to be on the part of the tax authorities.

But the adjustment will take time, and time means suffering. The only way to take the sting out of it is to slow down our expectations – though already there are voices in the air demanding immediate extra-parliamentary action to preserve jobs and force the creation of new ones. A great deal of the indignation must be excused, but without the restraint of some external moral standards we are liable to promote the end above the means. If the rival systems allow no chance for conscience to assert itself, then a substitute will have to be installed by the law, and that itself is of unreliable morality.

Is work itself a categorical imperative? It seems to me that, for the Christian, the real imperative is not to produce the maximum output, but to serve one's neighbour to the best of one's ability and that this may be done in ways that do not fall into the categories of union or management.

CHAPTER TWELVE

God Made the Land

I smell angry reactions ahead, so let me declare my interest in this matter. As between peasants, workers and intellectuals, I fall into the camp of the intellectuals. I spend most of my time in the city, I own no land, I neither hunt, shoot nor fish and there has not been a farmer in my family since a Manx great-grandfather died in 1879. But I do retreat to the far west of Cornwall whenever I can, I have a daughter there who supervises a herd of cows with the aid of a computer, and I suppose I share the English nostalgia for rural life and the curious assumption that the countryside belongs to all of us, whether or not we live and work there, for it is where we all came from.

Farmers – my target for today – have developed a remarkable tolerance towards this arrogant sentimentality. The countryside is their home, their workshop and largely their creation, but the rest of us claim the right to walk all over it, stare at it, sit on it and then start laying down the law about how it should be managed. Few other occupations have to put up with so much peeping and prying, so much amateur criticism and official manipulation as the farming community.

I am not trying to depict the farmer as a downtrodden innocent. He was there before the steam engine was dreamed of and he will be there when the microchip is out of date. Not for nothing has he the reputation of crying ruin while he takes delivery of his new Mercedes; and the government he complains about is the government which subsidizes him and picks up the tab for his over-production. Nothing I shall say in his defence should be taken as denying the fact that there are bad, callous, unscrupulous farmers, as there are journalists, motor-car dealers and double-glazing men. But there are two big differences between them: newspapers, cars and glass have never had the same romantic appeal as the land, and they are not represented by the National Farmers' Union – probably the most skilful lobby in Britain. I think it has a good case, and it does not miss a trick in making it.

You have only to riffle through the NFU's extensive literature to get an idea of the moral criticisms now facing the farmer. There are booklets entitled 'He cares . . .' showing a farmer standing guard over a rolling vista of crops and hedges, brochures on animal welfare unpromisingly called 'The case for cages', and articles about NFU members offering sanctuary to badgers and corn-buntings. Crossly, the Union complains[1]: 'Farmers are under vociferous and emotional attacks by misguided and misinformed critics for allegedly destroying our rural heritage and wildlife. The reverse is the case. Farmers are cooperating wherever possible in schemes which integrate practical methods of conservation with maximum food production.' Cynics note the 'possible . . . practical . . . maximum . . .' and demand that some outside authority, not the farmer himself, should define and enforce them.

Few other countries, if any, have made such a moral and aesthetic issue out of farming. Some have blamed it, without really explaining it, on the Romantic Movement in British literature and painting: on the highly selective views of the landscape by people like Constable and Wordsworth. No other nation has made its landscape seem so intimate, lovable and almost human; but then its very scale and the way it has been settled have made it look more like a garden than a wilderness. You cannot treat the American prairies

[1] NFU *Insight* No. 132, 26th January 1981

or the Russian steppes as a pet. Nor, because of their very size, are they so precious to their owners.

And because the British were the first to pollute their land with an industrial revolution, they may have become the first to react backwards to the rural life their great-grandfathers left, and to have felt all the more betrayed at discovering that farming, too, had become an industry with its own forms of pollution. The sort of people who were appalled by smog, nuclear fallout and effluent in the city drinking water had expected something better of the farmyards and cornfields. They did not want to accept that town and country were not alternative worlds – one fallen and the other innocent – but both parts of the same world, the same economy.

The religious find it particularly hard to accept this, for they tend to have in their hearts a vision of the country based upon the early chapters of Genesis: a near-Eden, stocked by God and husbanded by Man as a sacred charge. That is, in fact, the moral basis of the matter. No farmer who is a Christian can put his private property rights before the duty he owes to his Maker which is, above all, to serve his fellow men. But, immediately, things become much more complicated than not using chemical sprays and fertilisers, leaving hedges for the birds to nest in and raising calves out of doors.

This is not Eden, it is an economy of markets and there are a great many more people to feed than Adam could have managed. The NFU would like to remind you that every British farmworker feeds fifty people, that British farms supply sixty percent of all the food we eat and seventy-five percent of all the foodstuffs that could be produced in our climate. Furthermore (it argues) productivity has been rising continuously since World War II and the real cost to the citizen of almost all our foodstuffs has gone down. None of this would have been imaginable without intensive modern methods; and with the world's population increasing, we

dare not put the clock back. It is all very well to talk about
the natural stewardship of Eden, and even to adopt it on a
limited private scale, but it will not supply the cities with
eggs at 70p a dozen.

The attack upon this kind of argument branches out in
many directions, some of which I shall pursue. For I can
hardly maintain that we must not allow systems to go
unchallenged and then let this one through on the nod. Can
we – in the interests of cheap food – countenance the
destruction of the landscape, the poisoning of wild life and
the degradation of livestock? The answer is not necessarily a
resounding No. Maybe we *can* countenance it (in practice,
we seem to reckon it the lesser evil), but maybe it is not the
evil some suppose.

For a start, no kind of farming is 'natural'. Any sort of
clearing, digging and sowing of selected species is an interference with nature. The only truly 'natural' way of life
would be to gather fruits, roots and berries from the wild.
Nor is any of the landscape that we see in Britain today
purely natural: it has all been interfered with. Left to itself,
nature would produce a countryside very different from
that we so much admire, and the most conservative conser-
vationist is actually trying to prevent nature – as well as the
farmer – from taking its course.

Eighty percent of Britain is farmed to some degree, and
as the demands made upon farming have changed, so has
the landscape. I know one part of West Cornwall where the
field patterns are unaltered from Iron Age times; but many
of the hedges whose disappearance elsewhere is being
lamented date only from the enclosures of the 19th century,
made in violation of the commons and open fields. There is
a stretch of Berkhamsted Common, where I was brought
up, which was a wilderness of gorse and bracken until it was
ploughed up in a 'Dig for Victory' campaign forty years
ago, and has remained so ever since. When charcoal was in
demand, woods and coppices were there to earn their keep,

while moors, coverts, bogs and river banks owed as much to the demands of sporting landlords as to the chances of nature. Unpalatably to some, a countryside laid out for hunting, shooting and fishing is the very environment that wild life needs. The landscape, in short, has always been changing, has always worked for Man, and when people clamour to preserve the traditional English countryside they mean that they want to freeze it in a particular period, not necessarily the one that works for today.

But the counter-attack comes that farmers are greedy and insensitive and that only the law can stop them from destroying a beauty which cannot be priced on the market. There probably are such farmers, indeed I know two or three who abuse their land disgracefully: their neighbours know them as *bad* farmers. I know many more who are quite the opposite and are as devoted to their views as any tourist – more so, because they have lived with them all their lives and mean to pass them on as a living to their children.

But it is the fashion now to conserve the past – buildings as well as landscapes – partly, I suspect, because we have so little confidence in our own ability to do things as well. So about half our agricultural land is designated and restricted in one way or another, often to the confusion of the farmer who is not sure whether society is signalling him to grow more at all costs or to put the view or the flora and fauna first. Sometimes the owner is actually paid *not* to use his property as he might like; which sounds fair in theory but opens up some curious possibilities of extension. Why am I not compensated, for example, for preserving the inconvenient window-frames of my Edwardian home, or for refraining from writing pornographic novels? On the other hand, many farmers feel they are being got at by people who do not understand country life, make no real contribution to it, but are driven by class envy and have not really thought out what it is they are trying to conserve.

The mutual bitterness rises to a climax over the animal kingdom. Whether it is hens in cages, calves in crates or foxes pursued on horseback, there is no surer way to bring out the people-haters than to provoke the animal-lovers. It so happens that this is not an issue which I, personally, feel obliged to put high on my moral agenda – but it is enough to say *that* to be branded for ever after as a vivisectionist and a torturer, not fit to share the earth with fur and feather. It is no defence to quote Genesis once more, with its meat-eating and sacrifices and subjugation of the beasts to Man. That is seen as a kind of barbarous paganism. The vision now is that of an interdependent Creation over which Man has no right to claim the mastery and which he must respect rather than exploit.

Exploit, of course, is a poisoned word. Genesis at least shows Man being licensed to make use of what is around him and there is no suggestion anywhere in the Bible that God disapproves of him doing so. As to the suggestion that Man is no more than an equal member of the animal kingdom, this seems to me an absurd evasion. I would argue that Man has a duty towards the birds, beasts and fishes – and to all created nature – but that this cannot stand in the way of his duty to *use* that creation for purposes that forward the welfare of Man. That this welfare matters supremely to God seems to me of the essence of religious faith. So far as we can tell, we alone know God and have the power of moral choice; and we alone (though many good, kind people refuse to accept this implication of the Church's teaching) have the promise of immortality. There is still no evidence, whatever the mathematical probabilities and the fantasies of science fiction, that there is any creature like Man in this or any other Universe.

I shall probably be accused of building up a case for unbridled 'speciesism'. I mean no such thing. I do indeed believe that Man has priority in the Universe, and is intended to by God. But that priority is not the priority of a self-made conqueror, it is that of one appointed as steward or representative of the Creator Himself and it bears with it the heavy duty of caring for the rest of His creation. All too clearly Man has failed in his duty time and again. But he is forgiven if he repents. He cannot lay down the burden, and he should not retreat into pretending he is no more than just another animal.

We cannot deny Man's crimes: the annihilation of other species, the deforestation of vast areas, the plundering of mineral wealth. I suspect that the Holy Spirit itself, which does sometimes take the guise of economic forces, has been moving with some effect to check the worst of these excesses; and I have the support of a recent Archbishop of Canterbury who thanked God for acting 'through His servant Sheikh Yamani of OPEC' to chastise us for our waste of oil. But I think we must be careful to distinguish between uses of nature which are absolutely wrong and those which only become wrong by being taken too far. Enough is enough – it is too much that is sinful.

Where the use of animals is concerned, it seems to me far better to raise them deliberately for the purpose of our use than to pluck them out of nature and risk destroying its balance. Not that even our wild game can be said, any more, to be in natural balance: in a country like Britain the entire ecology has been so 'managed' for centuries that we are obliged to go on managing it – culling deer, trapping coypu, hunting foxes to name only a few examples. And if this sort of management also appeals to some people's hunting instincts, how can those who do not share them repress them? As I say, I do not share them myself, but I do not find hunting-and-shooting people to be morally corrupted by their activities and I do find many of those who oppose them to be infected by envies and hatreds which I cannot admire. Besides exaggerating the horrors of the hunt, they seem to me to miss both the purpose and spirit of these sports. The most bloodthirsty sentiments I ever heard came from a correspondent who was so obsessed with the total vileness of mankind, contrasted with the animals, that he ended his letter '. . . and I hope we are all wiped out by one great big beautiful H-bomb!' He had a curious reverence for life.

At the root of many protests against the farming of animals is the conviction that the eating of flesh is wrong. It is said to be disrespectful of life, which is seen as the absolute good. The process of slaughter is condemned as inhumane. The use of cereals and feedstuffs like maize and manioc is said to be wasteful and to deprive the Third World of calories so that the First World can wallow in proteins. It is said we would all be healthier, too, if we were to adopt vegetarian diets.

Some of this must be true. Wartime rationing proved that most of us do eat too much and that we do not need all the animal fats and meat we guzzle. With a new agricultural revolution we might be able to feed ourselves and have something over to send the world's undernourished: though both they and we would have to eat very differently from the way we eat now, and we would somehow have to devise a system for giving away quantities of food and yet finding the resources to grow more.

It is true that vegetarian peoples do not suffer from some of the diseases that afflict us. But they suffer from others, their diet is adapted to different conditions, and it is hard to believe that we would have achieved what we have by giving up meat. If we ceased to buy feedstuffs from the Third World, one wonders how else they would earn the money for the things they have to import. One wonders, also, where the line is to be drawn defining 'life' – whether a cut lettuce may not be shown to feel pain? More seriously, one wonders what many British farmers would grow if pigs, sheep and beef cattle were unsaleable. Milk is generally regarded as acceptable by vegetarians; but before a cow can give milk it has to give birth, and it is as likely to bear a male calf as a female. What else can you do with a bullock but eat it?

The fact is, the great majority of people in Britain enjoy eating meat and see nothing wrong in it. To them it is not a moral issue, even though they can hardly be innocent of what the meat is. I happen to be a pacifist; but I have to accept that other people see war as – at worst – a necessary evil, and although I may argue with them there are limits to my right to make them share my view. It is a matter of conscience. One may well wonder if the consciences of meat-eaters are adequately informed, whether they realize exactly how their meat is raised and killed and whether they would continue to eat it if they knew. Many of them might. I can only say that I am in favour of their knowing. Knowledge of this kind has already curbed much avoidable cruelty, and British farmers like to claim they have always been ready to adapt to changing views of what is humane – though they still have to make a living out of animals dying. I find them reluctant to call themselves unsentimental; they would probably explain that like doctors towards their patients, they have to be more detached and realistic than the rest of us would be.

That does not mean that crude market forces are the only things that move the farmer. But if ever there was a revulsion from eating meat and an overwhelming demand for beans and cereals, Britain's farming industry would simply be obliged to stop producing meat and cater for a vegetarian market. Goodness knows what would happen to all the bullocks. The point is, our farms grow meat not because farmers are bloodthirsty and enjoy taking life, but because most of us do not agree that all life is of equal status, because we choose to eat meat and are happy to pay the price. And an economy, because it is the result of an aggregation of choices, seldom expresses a coherent moral judgment.

The animal lobby, however, will remain unhappy about the way intensive farming handles such living crops as veal calves, porkers, broilers and battery hens; and few city folk who have seen some of these practices will dismiss the protests out of hand. The farming industry still has to argue strenuously to justify them, and where it has been able to modify them (for example, crated calves are going out of fashion) it has done so with some relief and usually the explanation that the new methods are also more efficient.

Farmers will always insist that a suffering animal does not thrive, so that it is in their commercial interest to see their beasts are happy. Whether a hen's happiness requires the liberty and choice we demand for ourselves, how long a life counts as thriving, and how far beasts experience mental suffering is hard to say. But certainly there are objective codes of practice, supervised by the Veterinary Service, which, the industry claims, ensure the welfare of its charges.

Is that enough? I have suggested that moral judgments involve the question 'What sort of person do I think I am?' And I have to confess that I am not the sort of person who could happily manage a battery-house. I know the arguments in its favour[2]: that hens in cages are freer from predators, parasites and disease; that they do not have to worry about getting their fair share of food or suffer from bullying, hysteria or inclement weather; that the eggs are collected clean and fresh and at half the price they would have been free range. Something like ninety-five percent of all the laying hens in the United Kingdom are kept in battery cages, but that still does not make me feel comfortable about them. For a hen can be a beautiful creature and I have seen few sights more pathetic than an ex-battery hen trying to adapt to the world of the farmyard. It shows, perhaps, that I, too, can be sentimental and unrealistic. At least I am glad to read of experiments with something called the 'aviary system' which combines deep litter with tiers of slatted floors and nesting boxes. It suggests to me that, for all the

2 *The Case for Cages* and *Sense or Sentiment*, NFU pamphlets

National Farmers' Union's huffing and puffing about the
recommendation of the Commons Select Committee that
cages be abolished, the industry's own conscience is far
from quiet. The same applies to its defence of calf-crating,
which it says has been 'considerably improved' and will
probably be replaced with a system of keeping groups of
calves in straw-yards. The NFU adds defiantly that this
shows how it *can* combine efficiency with welfare if it is left
without interference. And it takes an angry slap at militant
animal-lovers who invade farms to steal birds and animals –
'. . . particularly reprehensible because it can cause
immense harm to the stock they claim to be liberating,
causing panic and stress[3].

The issue of chemical fertilizers and pesticides produces
another thicket of defiance, self-justification and embarrassment. Add to it the pollution of watercourses with the
effluent from silage mounds and the slurry from enormous
pig and cow units (some of them producing as much
sewage as a medium-sized town), and it is hard to resist the
conclusion that *some* farmers have been careless and even
reckless about poisoning the environment. Even the NFU
admits that: 'For a brief period in the 1960s some farmers
were culprits.' It goes on to plead that they were often the
addicts of new techniques which they did not fully understand and that pollution was rare and no longer a serious
problem anywhere in Britain. To some extent farmers –
like doctors – have been swept off their feet by the chemical
companies and plead that if the official regulatory agencies
do not warn them of the dangers, how are they to know?
Today, they add, most chemicals are so expensive that
no one can afford to use them in any but the minimum
effective quantities. If farmer or consumer wish to confine
themselves to natural organic foods, they are welcome to.
But economically this cannot be more than a limited and
expensive fad.

[3] NFU background document, June 1982

There has been no such thing as natural farming since the Iron Age, and we can hardly go back to it unless we return to Iron Age levels of diet and population. The high-yielding breeds of cereals and vegetables we rely upon today are as remote from their natural ancestors as the motor-car from the chariot. One ran on organic fuel, the other on petro-chemicals, and without chemical fertilizers the North American prairies would not be able to bail out the rest of the world from its famines, or the paddy-fields of India to support a population which has doubled since the 1940s. It is not that farmers have flogged the old species beyond the limits of endurance, but that entirely new species have been developed requiring a richer diet themselves. Dung won't do; and, incidentally, there would be even less of that if we stopped eating meat.

Almost as important as the increase in fertility has been the decrease in wastage. Nobody much regrets the suppression of rats and mice (except, I suppose, the weasels and birds of prey), but few appreciate that without the use of pesticides our corn and potato crops would be lower by at least a quarter – cumulatively, far more. And so the calculations go on.

There is another calculation linking this story with my last two essays: for if we are to spend more as a society on creating work for the unemployed and elevating the poor, we shall only divert money from those purposes if we ban methods which enable the farmer to grow cheap food. Certainly we have to be careful not to equip him with tools that endanger us all, but we should not imagine that even the National Farmers' Union has been able to rig society entirely in its favour. If we suspect farmers of debauching our heritage, it is time to realize that the rest of us have been thoughtless about theirs.

The new romanticism about the countryside is not entirely sincere. Town folk expect it to be there for their pleasure, unspoilt (except by townspeople), but they are reluctant to spend much money for the privilege, and at the fall of a raindrop they will take off for the Mediterranean. The cult of the countryside feeds off our disgust with our decaying cities, but when we need more room for housing, factories, motorways and airports we steal it off the countryside at the rate of 50,000 acres a year, more than half of it good agricultural land. It is extremely hard, in Britain, to reclaim more than a fraction of this in the opposite direction.

Something like 650,000 people make their living from the land, not a powerful contingent in terms of voting or purchasing, but they can claim a contribution to our welfare way out of proportion to their numbers. Besides the food they produce (and after two World Wars we should feel very uncomfortable without that assurance) they provide a healthy complement to the urban side of our way of life, one which is easily kept in touch with by anyone who cares to. It is the town-*and*-country character of Britain that makes it so pleasant to live in.

Many of our well-to-do enjoy that to the utmost by living in the country and commuting to the towns, or by acquiring country cottages for part-time residence (as I must admit I have done myself). We part-timers like to claim that we rescue derelict properties from collapse or dress up rural slums whose tenants have rejected the back lanes anyway and gone to live in modern council estates. There is more truth in this than chauvinist cottage-burners will admit; but the incomers must agree, for their part, that they do not contribute much to country life. Nor have local government reforms, which have left parish councils – so active forty years ago – with little power in their own communities, and often put country populations at the mercy of urban councillors who neither know nor care about them. Where a local authority does develop a conscience about the countryside it is liable (farmers complain) to take the form of treating it like a museum and banning developments which, in a town, would be welcomed with open arms.

The country, of course, is not the town. Some local authorities are understandably not keen to find obscure hamlets filling up with elderly retired people, or even young families, demanding expensive public services; and I have known farmers who were not above turning their pig-sties into holiday chalets or building a bungalow for a mythical agricultural labourer and then putting it on the market to all comers. There is no denying, either, that many new farm buildings are an insult to the landscape. The trouble is, modern farming calls for something more like a factory shed than a granite barn with a hipped roof.

The British philosophy that the countryside is for every-one, and that you may trespass anywhere provided you do no damage, is probably unique and farmers know better than to resist it. They complain about picnic rubbish, about dogs worrying their livestock, about gates left open, fires started and equipment vandalized, but in general they tolerate a freedom for all that I have met nowhere else in the world. But it makes their operations more difficult, especially when footpaths and national parks are designated over their property. I have written enough to show that I do not believe all the cries of hardship that farmers utter, but I do think it is time the rest of us paid more for the pleasure we take in what is, to a very large extent, somebody else's handiwork.

And if we believe – as many of us say we do – in rural communities as a healthy way of life, perhaps as something more of us would like to get back to, then we should contemplate what is happening to them before it is too late. Partly because machinery has replaced so many labourers, partly because the work is hard and not highly paid, and partly, too, because no alternative jobs have arisen, popula-tion has been slipping away from the rural areas into the towns. It has been happening, I suppose, for at least two centuries; but today, just as there is some hope of reversing it, the countryside finds itself with fewer services and facilities – shops, post offices, schools and buses – than there were fifty years ago. Working class country people, whom we still need if the countryside *is* to work, risk being driven into the ranks of the powerless and ineffectual. They resent this, and do not see why they should be denied the conveniences that town people take for granted. Yet only the well-to-do commuter can afford to overcome the deprivation, the lack of transport, the closing of village schools, the distance from employment and medical services. And this commuter is not responsible for, or responsive to, the land.

It would be wrong for the conscientious person, especially the Christian, to assume that the man–made city is bad and the God-made country good. There is a long tradition of the City of God and of building to the Glory of God. In any case, a community is its people rather than its walls and streets. On the other hand, we have seen how Man has helped to shape and alter the countryside God gave him. But, at the risk of sounding banal, only God can make a tree or a cow or an ear of corn, and the country year repeats the sacrificial process of living things dying so that new things may rise and live. Man has a special relationship, a special responsibility among nature, and I would say that, whether or not he observes it faithfully, what the farmer is called upon to do is essentially worshipful. He is tending forces which he can modify and even control, but which are beyond his powers to create. Although he cannot afford to be too romantic about it, he is also responsible for the *sacramental* business of feeding his fellow men and women. He is certainly as sinful as the next person. He, too, is caught up in impersonal structures and systems which are increasingly dominated by interests which are not of the countryside: the interests of the rest of us. I think the farmer must do his utmost to remember whose creation, ultimately, he is caring for; but the rest of us must remember that it is often our demands that shout louder.

CHAPTER THIRTEEN

Whose Life
in Whose Hands?

I wish I knew less about Intensive Care Units, and what it is like to lie there, wired up and plugged in, willing my own blip across the monitor screen and pondering, drowsily, that if this is the end it is less painful than I had expected but disappointingly impersonal. A friend of mine woke up in an ICU to hear somebody saying, 'Don't worry, Mr Phipps, you're on a life-support machine *and I'm just switching off . . .*'

Life is never quite the same once you have been near to death, and I, for one, am very grateful for the intensive care and that nobody definitively switched me off. I owe my birth, my health, my sanity and my continued existence to the skill of my doctors; but I cannot help sharing some of the unease that we found with farming: that man is presuming too much against nature, departing too far from what is natural: that, once again, the individual is being swept along by the system without the power to make his own choices.

In fifty, perhaps twenty, years' time my descendants may be genetically planned by a computer, assembled from a bank, conceived in a dish, vetted and adjusted before delivery, re-equipped with spare parts as they proceed along life's motorway, and finally unplugged when they fail to score the minimum QUOLPs (or Quality of Life Points). Admittedly a lot of this is only the development of what goes on today. Admittedly we have always been too fearful of advances like anaesthesia, immunization and blood transfusion which have turned out to be substantial blessings. But we now seem to be going beyond merely caring for the life which 'the Lord giveth and the Lord taketh away' and to be appropriating the giving and taking to ourselves. If 'we' meant all of us and all of us were wise, such an appropriation might even be seen as an extension of moral choice; but most of us are out of our depth already and fearful of becoming sheep to the medical profession. By the end of the century, what shall we be allowed to die of? The question is less fantastic than it may sound, for already whole diseases have been virtually abolished and there is no reason why the process should not accelerate.

Modern medicine threatens to become yet another system dividing the two nations, the well-to-do, educated and powerful from the poor, ignorant and powerless. It is not so much the money that counts as the social and educational know-how. One knows from experience that by reading, listening and demanding explanations one *can* assert choices over one's treatment, and that this tends to be a prerogative of the middle-class, just as much in the National Health Service as under private care.

Another friend of mine once found, on the chart at the foot of her hospital bed, a note saying: 'This patient is highly intelligent and should be told as little as possible'; but generally that is *not* considered the right attitude, if only because a patient who understands what is going on and why is likely to cooperate and get better quicker. A patient who is lied to will almost certainly find out in the end. Thus the best modern medical schools stress the importance of communicating with patients. Oddly enough, however, a doctor is not obliged by law to tell a patient the truth about his or her condition – unless it has been made clear that legal arrangements like a will depend on the answer[1].

At this point I must make what may sound like an outrageous assertion: I do not believe that doctors are much

---

[1] I am obliged throughout to *The Dictionary of Medical Ethics (Revised)*, A. S. Duncan & Others; Darton, Longman & Todd, 1981

bothered by ethical problems, and perhaps it is just as well. They can hardly tend their patients while racked with doubts. Whatever their philosophy, they try to bring comfort and healing as best they can, and they are more likely to be disturbed by what society is doing to their patients – housing, feeding and educating them badly, or providing inadequate medical facilities for them – than they are by problems of pure ethics.

More than most professions, more than journalists, even, doctors close ranks and preserve solidarity when criticised. But they should remember that what they do has profound moral implications for the rest of us, and that any group with power deserves to be monitored lest it develop into an unthinking system. My intention in this chapter is not to try particular cases, but to raise some of the general issues and principles affecting the climate of medicine, in the hope that we may all understand it better and, if necessary, change it.

Thus there are certainly grounds for accusing some – perhaps too many – doctors of failing to communicate with their patients properly so that the patients can make choices. Some doctors plead that they simply have not the time, or that their patients are too ill-educated to understand – both of which are reproaches to the community as much as to the doctor. Other practitioners are afraid of getting too involved in their patients' personal difficulties and would rather treat them as purely physical cases. This may be inadequate medicine, but it has to be admitted that (rather like the farmer with his livestock) a certain detachment must be preserved for the doctor's survival. It is hard, too, for the doctor to avoid being put on a pedestal by the patients themselves, and he becomes still more unreachable if, like many other professionals, he falls into the habit of talking specialized jargon. This is not just a personal problem: medicine as a whole finds it difficult to explain simply to the public what it is up to, though it is quick to complain if the mass media oversimplify things, creating either panic or the expectation of miracles. Either way, the result is an atmosphere of mutual suspicion and contempt where there should be one of cooperation for the public good. Once again, how can the media publish the truth if those who know it won't tell it?

From the public's point of view the classic problem of truth-telling is presented by the patient suffering from a terminal illness. Should his doctor tell him the truth? But it is not a question that can be answered 'always' or 'never', for it is always presented in a particular case, never in the abstract; and the doctor's supreme duty is not to follow an abstract principle regardless of consequences, but to care for (a Christian would unashamedly say – love) the human being in his charge.

In some cases that love will best be served by stating the facts; but in others, where the patient might be thrown into even greater suffering by knowing them, it may not. Even this is far too insensitive. For a start, what *are* the facts? Not necessarily as stark as, 'You will be dead of cancer before the end of the month' – and that would be a brutally unloving way of putting it, even if it were one hundred percent certain. There are ways of putting these things which a doctor learns – some, inevitably, better than others. There is timing, building up the truth by stages, the approach will vary with the sort of patient involved, how much he knows or can understand, how ready he is spiritually for death, how much he or his family can stand at one time. Many doctors can tell how ready their patients are by the questions they ask, and some doctors are actually told by their patients, 'I know I am dying'. It is not a matter that can be laid down by regulation and certainly not by an outsider like me.

That also applies to *some* aspects of the confidentiality expected between doctor and patient. In principle, just as a doctor ought not to lie to a patient about his condition, so he ought not to betray the patient's secrets. But there must be cases where either his concern for the patient's wellbeing (say, a young girl trying to hide an abortion from her parents) or his knowledge that a patient is a danger to society (say, a murderer) must drive the doctor to find a way round that secrecy if he can. In some cases – a notifiable infectious disease or a patient who is insane – the law allows or requires the doctor to break confidence; or he may be ordered to do so under examination in court. But in general, secrecy is safeguarded by law, suggesting that our society is more anxious about that than it is about truth-telling.

The doctor, however, has more than his own conscience on the one hand and the law on the other to offer him moral guidance. Originating as a religious practice, passed down through a brotherhood of initiates, western medicine has a traditional code of ethics enshrined in the Hippocratic tradition from ancient Greece. The profession still endeavours to uphold that tradition by policing its own behaviour; partly, I suspect, because it knows all too well how complex its moral problems may be and does not want them to be unworkably regulated by outsiders; but partly because it still retains an essentially religious approach to life itself, a sense of its own priesthood over God's gift.

Some may complain that I have already prejudiced the argument by introducing the name of the Lord at all; that once you start putting a halo round life and presenting it as something holy lent to us by some higher being, it becomes impossible to talk about it objectively and realistically. It can (such critics might argue) even brush aside people's rights over their lives.

That could equally apply to a humanistic view of the sanctity of life. But as a Christian and a believer that life *is* a divine gift and that God has a will for each one, I have to agree that His presence does put things in a different light. But I would claim it was the real and objective light, a great deal less subject to distortion than the secular light. Nor, since God wills human welfare, is it any the less humanist, as an examination of the Hippocratic Oath will show.

After invoking Apollo and the gods, the physician binds himself into a family relationship with his teachers, students and colleagues. He promises to give treatment solely for the good of his patients, never to harm them. He will help nobody to commit suicide, he will not prescribe drugs for abortion, and he will leave surgery to the specialists in that art. He will lead a pure life, never seduce a patient of either sex, and never reveal personal secrets learned in the exercise of his profession.

Few doctors take such an oath today. Down the centuries its details were often varied, and it is argued that since it originated with a particular sect of healers it was never meant to be taken as a code for all, let alone a law. At first sight the medical profession of today would seem to have turned its back on the part concerning abortion, though one must set that against the overall dedication to the good of the patient. The Hippocratic Oath is not exempt from the dilemma awaiting all attempts to codify ethics – that most moral issues involve more than one question, and the problem is – Which takes priority? There is no better place to see this than at the start of life itself.

But we had better be careful about what we mean by 'life', and even more careful about such a dominating phrase as 'the sanctity of life'. For all its Christian roots, the western attitude has always been that while individual existence is to be valued *extremely* it is not to be valued *supremely*. Most people still justify going to war, in the last resort, and it seems that many would justify capital punishment as well. Personally I regret both, believing that I, at least, have no right to take life. But what – that has any meaning – can I say to those who believe they have a positive duty to do so? And whatever my stand on those issues, I have to accept that it is not possible to preserve all life, all the time, at all costs. We preserve more and more for

longer and longer, and what we *can* do affects our view of
what we *ought* to do. But we still act as if there were a
hierarchy of life and a price for life which we are prepared to
pay in lives. The honourable tradition of 'women and children first' implies that men are prepared to be sacrificed.
Rather less honourably we enjoy the convenience of the
motor-car sooner than abolish it and save the lives it takes.

Meanwhile the Christian's view of life and its value is
bound to be influenced by his belief that it is not the end:
that while it is a great and precious gift it is only the
preparation for a higher life to come. This gives nobody the
right to dispose of another's life, but it also means that death
is not the tragedy to be avoided at all costs which it must
often seem to the non-believer. Equally, suffering should
appear rather differently to the Christian. He is not taught (I
think) that it is good in itself, but it can be redemptive: that
is, something good can be brought out of the evil so that the
last state of the sufferer can be better than the first. Quite
recently, a non-believing friend of mine, dying of cancer,
was transformed by the gradual realization that this was *not*
the end, that there *was* something more.

But still, what *is* life? And if we can only claim the most
exceptional right to kill an aggressor or murderer, can we
possibly claim to abort an unborn child who has done no
harm? Let us leave aside the most obvious hard cases, where
the mother's life is in danger or the child is known to be
grossly handicapped. Let us leave aside also the arguments
about reducing the deaths from back-street abortions and
saving children from being born unwanted. Let us suppose
we are talking of the woman who, after thorough con-
sideration, is simply not prepared to have her baby and who
satisfies all the requirements of the law. The abortion may
be legal, but is it right?

Again there is no such thing as the abstract case, and I am
not attracted to the theory that there are large numbers of
women – perhaps more than a hundred thousand a year in

Britain – casually disposing of their pregnancies, without regret, as an alternative to practising contraception. There may be some like this, but for most there *is* regret and quite often sorrow. Abortion is distasteful and, after the early weeks, no trivial matter. I would say it is an evil, just as war is an evil, and like war I would rather see the need for it stopped by preventive methods than have it come to pass. Like war, abortion is a confession of failure, and those who conscientiously feel they must resort to it have the duty to do so humbly, humanely and swiftly and then to repent, seek forgiveness and be resurrected.

Which is of little comfort to the unborn child. But when is it a child – when is it life? Few people who have seen the remarkable Swedish film of a foetus developing in the womb, or who have noted the diminishing age at which premature babies can now survive, can feel happy about the lateness at which abortions are sometimes performed. There are plenty of horror stories in the pro-life literature – not all of them true – but the fact is there can be no objective definition of when a foetus is a person with rights which can be said to match those of its mother. There is life (of a kind, and given the right conditions ahead) from the moment the fertilised egg is implanted in the womb, or perhaps when the sperm penetrates the egg: but there is life of a kind, also, in the egg and the sperm separately. If it is pure life, or the chance of it, that we are championing, then we should ban birth control and maximise copulation. If conscience and reason together draw the line at that, as they do even for most Roman Catholics today, then we have to grant that life may legitimately be prevented from developing. A moral law, such as the Roman Church's against artificial contraception, does not necessarily cease to be valid just because people no longer observe it; but when one falls into neglect like this, the Church might ask itself whether it has informed the people's conscience correctly, or whether it is the people's conscience which is now the better informed.

We should not apply that too glibly to the matter of abortion, but it does seem that the public conscience accepts it, and since it does, the authorities – taking the best advice they can get – can only nominate a point beyond which 'life' is held to begin and abortion becomes killing. Plainly we should 'err on the side of life', as we should with babies who are born handicapped, but if we can accept neither the Vatican line of an absolute right to life nor the extreme feminist one of a woman's absolute right over her own body, then we can only make the best guess we can and beg forgiveness if we are proved wrong. What we can hardly do is *compel* women to bear their children. We have to live with consequences of our choices – the noble ones as well as the ignoble – and the prospect of bringing up a hundred thousand babies a year who would otherwise have been aborted is not one which I think the community is prepared to contemplate.

Many of the moral problems attributed to medicine are not really those of practising doctors and surgeons at all, but of scientific researchers like the pharmacologists and genetic engineers. If these scientists make discoveries which are clearly beneficial to patients, doctors will use them and we shall all applaud. Already we are applauding the test-tube baby technique, and most of us have recovered from our initial fright over organ transplants. Quite apart from the existing codes covering experiments, it is hard to see why anyone should waste time and money producing monsters. The greater danger is that the exploitation of new discoveries by business may get out of hand; as it has done, here and there, with the use of antibiotics and hormones in animal feed. Nor is business the only exploiter of medicine: the armed forces and policemen of the world exploit it, too, from bacteriological warfare to injections for dissidents.

The doctor cannot keep clear of politics any more than he can help breathing the air: it is the environment in which he lives, like the rest of us. Like the rest of us he has to make a living, and he will certainly have views on how society rewards him. I am not going to argue the case here of private medicine *versus* the National Health Service: my own experience, which includes a cancer in the family, is that private medicine had no advantages to offer. Long before the NHS, British doctors recognised and practised their duty to the poor, and none I know of today thinks the nation takes its Health Service seriously enough. We are evidently *not* 'all socialists now', but at least our doctors are far from being the wholehearted money-minters some of their American colleagues have become. To most Americans 'socialised medicine' is satanic. At the same time, I have to admit that the doctor who treated my family in the United States was deeply devoted to their welfare, and far less likely to pull rank on a layman than most English doctors. But this, perhaps, was as much a national characteristic as a result of the fact that I was paying the bill.

What we demand of our doctors is not necessarily what they would like to be doing. There are bound to be the occasional dramas, but ideally any doctor would prefer to be keeping people healthy rather than treating their illnesses. The rest of us, however, persist in regarding our GP as a repairman to be visited when things go wrong, and the system is largely geared to that.

It would seem commonsense to demand a massive transfer of resources to health education and preventive medicine – checkups for all every few months, classes and clinics, immunizations, campaigns to encourage exercise, ban alcohol and tobacco and get people to eat sensibly: but the fact is, this would not replace our existing expenditure on health, it would simply add to it. And if it worked it would add more still because people would live longer and have to be looked after in old age. All of which might be admirable, but it would face us once more with the question 'Where will the money come from?' The existing 'repairman' approach to medicine has its faults, but it is relatively economical and concentrates resources on those who are actually suffering.

We cannot deny that most of us do incredibly stupid things to our bodies, are our own worst enemies. I do not smoke, but I certainly eat and drink too much – of the wrong things – and I take far too little exercise and sit in the wrong shaped chairs. There are millions like me, and there are others worse still who lead such intolerable lives that they take to drugs or end up with overdoses (now the commonest cause of admission to many hospitals). It is a scandal, and I am surprised the medical profession is not tempted to throw down its stethoscopes and refuse to treat us unless we pull ourselves together. We at last managed to overcome our virile inhibitions against making seat-belts compulsory; but we still won't stand up against the brewers, distillers and tobacco merchants, perhaps because if we banned their wares the state would lose the revenue with which to pay for the cirrhosis, lung cancer and heart disease they cause.

All of which is good rhetoric but not so morally straight-forward as it looks. Even if we accept the evidence against things like butter, sugar, salt, tobacco and alcohol, we must still come to terms with compulsion. Choice, we know, is necessary for us to survive as moral beings. Some choices we eliminate because they impose intolerable burdens upon others. But how far can society go in narrowing down the choices without replacing right and wrong with conform-ing and nonconforming – and what would that do both to the public as a whole and to those who defined and enforced conformity?

You may argue that the burden of an alcoholic falls not just upon himself but upon everyone round him; that he may actually become a danger to his community. But is that a good enough reason for banning alcohol to everyone? And if we do that, where do we stop, and who, once more, is to decide this? To its own credit, the medical profession as a whole has not rushed to appoint itself the moral censor of the nation. The right to drink oneself to death (hopefully in a civilized manner) remains; as does the right to take one's own life in any manner one wishes. Would that fewer people felt driven to avail themselves of it.

I believe that suicide is wrong, unless, conceivably, it is a service or sacrifice for others. But I can see it is hard to argue this without assuming that God has a will for us which we may not be able to discern. Suicides often persuade themselves that their survivors will be better off without them, but the survivors seldom agree. They are left with the burden of forgiving not only the suicide but themselves.

Death is medicine's last chance to be of service to us, and I think it is a pity that some doctors feel their duty must lie in defeating death and keeping the patient alive. The challenge may lie in the opposite direction – in making death and the patient agreeable friends. Here is another commonplace: but we all have to die some time and later is not always better than sooner. We are grateful, of course, that fathers now survive to see their children grow up, that very few mothers die in childbirth and few families have that lost generation of infants that never grew up, recorded on our great-grandparents' tombstones. The picture that haunts us today, though, is of old folk vegetating meaninglessly in geriatric wards, wondering who will turn off the switch. 'Doctor, what are you going to let me die of? When is the euthanasia man coming . . .'

Pathetic, exaggerated cases make bad law. Once more, the matter of dying is not one for rules and regulations or even guidelines from the ministry. Doctor and patient must ask themselves – What are the choices? What sort of person do I think I am? I am pretty sure that the sort of person who specializes in helping the elderly to kill themselves is the last to be trusted near them. It is one thing to seek satisfaction in extending life – quite another to seek it in ending life. The impression I gain from experienced doctors is that time and again they use their judgment and knowledge of the patient *not* to extend life pointlessly. 'Thou shalt not kill but needst not strive officiously to keep alive' is not a bad way of putting it, and it is pretty fair Christian theology also. Of course it would be intolerable if the public received the impression that doctors were in the business of 'switching off' people who were not worth bothering about, and as far back as the Hippocratic Oath the medical profession has sought to prohibit the notion. This may become an obsession in a large hospital where junior staff feel obliged to show their skill to the uttermost and where the patient and his family are not in close understanding with them. But there does come a point when the Hippocratic dedication to 'the good of my patient' must call for a release, a letting go, and it is not good, caring medicine to delay it when there is no hope. The specialized treatment of pain, especially in hospices, makes it increasingly possible for people to die without humiliating distress; and it is this, rather than 'jumping the gun' which ought to be the hope of the fearful. To wish not to be a burden to others may look admirable at first sight; but a society which applauds it and then comes to expect it is on the way to becoming inhuman.

Whether to conceive life, whether to bear it, maintain it and eventually terminate it, and what part the medical profession should play in these decisions, have been the subject of this final essay. As before, we have seen that the problems are much less those of the professionals in the field than of society as a whole, or rather of those of us in the society who are prepared to assert our duty to choose.

As in other fields, the professionals evolve their codes of conduct which are workable and with which they feel comfortable: very often they incorporate an element of self-defence, of: 'This is what we do and have always done.' But if the professionals may claim to be caught up in their system, it is still a system which cannot survive unless it satisfies the rest of us, that depends upon our demand and our response. It is only fair that we should understand the pressures upon the professionals, whether they are businessmen, soldiers, doctors, politicians or journalists. But we still have the duty – as you know, I am less keen upon rights – to listen to their explanations and then say: 'But that is not what we want – we want *this* . . .' We may then have to consider the implications of what we *do* want, and to lower our sights.

But at least we will have exerted our God-given free will, we will have tried to choose, we will have tried to be fully human.

Further Reading

For those who would like to pursue any particular topic further, I offer the following selection of titles under the chapters to which they relate.   G.P.

Chapter 1 (Moral Philosophy)

D. Brown, *Choices – Ethics and the Christian*, Blackwell 1983.
J. M. Gustafson, *Theology and Ethics*, Blackwell 1981.
R. Hare, *Moral Thinking*, OUP 1981.
J. L. Houlden, *Ethics and the New Testament*, Mowbrays 1979.
J. Mackie, *Ethics*, Penguin 1977.

Chapter 2 (Warfare)

R. Ardrey, *The Territorial Imperative*, Fontana 1969.
G. Best, *Humanity in Warfare*, Weidenfeld 1980.
L. Bramson & G. W. Goethals (eds.), *War*, Basic Books 1968.
B. Paskins & M. Dockrill, *The Ethics of War*, Duckworth 1979.
M. Walzer, *Just and Unjust Wars*, Penguin 1980.

Chapter 3 (Violence and Crime)

B. Crozier, *A Theory of Conflict*, Hamish Hamilton 1974.
A. Curle, *True Justice*, Quaker Home Service 1981.
R. Harries, *Should a Christian Support Guerrillas?*, Anselm Books 1982.

G. Priestland, *The Future of Violence*, Hamish Hamilton 1974.

G. Sorel, *Reflections on Violence*, Collier Macmillan 1970.

I. Taylor & others, *The New Criminology*, Routledge & Kegan Paul 1973.

Wyndham Place Trust, *Violence in Great Britain* (report) 1980.

Chapter 4 (Business)

J. K. Galbraith, *The New Industrial State*, Houghton Mifflin 1967.

G. McClelland, *And a new Earth*, Quaker Home Service 1976.

R. Preston, *Religions and the Persistence of Capitalism*, SCM Press 1979.

R. H. Tawney, *Religion and the Rise of Capitalism*, Penguin 1969.

Chapter 5 (Politics)

S. Hampshire (ed.), *Public and Private Morality*, Cambridge 1978.

P. Hinchcliff, *Holiness and Politics*, Darton Longman & Todd 1982.

D. B. Meyer, *The Protestant Search for Political Realism*, Greenwood 1973.

E. R. Norman, *Christianity and the World Order*, OUP 1979.

D. Thomson (ed.), *Political Ideas*, Pelican 1975.

Chapter 6 (Family and Sex)

J. Dominian, *Marriage, Faith and Love*, Darton Longman & Todd 1981.

M. Furlong, *Divorce: One Woman's View*, Mothers' Union 1981.

Marriage Commission, Church of England, *Marriage and the Church's Task*, CIO 1978.

F. Mount, *The Subversive Family*, Cape 1982.
F. Lake, *Clinical Theology*, Darton Longman & Todd 1966.
P. Coleman, *Christian Attitudes to Homosexuality*, SPCK 1980.

Chapter 7 (The Media)

G. Priestland, *The Dilemmas of Journalism*, Lutterworth 1979.
J. Tunstall, *Media Sociology*, Constable 1970 (and other writings).
J. Whale, *The Half-shut Eye*, Macmillan 1969.
J. Whale, *Journalism and Government*, Macmillan 1972.
A. Quicke, *Tomorrow's Television*, Lion Publishing 1976.

Chapter 8 (The Church)

C. Edward Barker, *The Church's Neurosis*, Rider 1975.
Doctrine Commission, Church of England, *Believing in the Church*, SPCK 1981.
H. Küng, *On Being a Christian*, Collins 1977, Fount 1978.
F. Nietzsche, *Twilight of the Idols etc.*, Penguin 1972.
G. Priestland, *Who Needs the Church?*, St Andrew Press 1983.

Chapter 9 (Luxury)

J. K. Galbraith, *The Affluent Society*, Penguin 1962.
New Testament throughout.
E. F. Schumacher, *Small is Beautiful*, Abacus/Sphere 1974.
V. Packard, *The Status Seekers*, Penguin 1961.

Chapter 10 (The Poor)

K. Coates & R. Silburn, *Poverty – The Forgotten Englishmen*, Pelican 1981.
D. Donnison, *The Politics of Poverty*, Martin Robertson 1982.

S. Rowntree & G. R. Lavers, *Poverty and the Welfare State*, Longmans 1951.
P. Townsend, *Poverty in the United Kingdom*, Penguin 1979.

Chapter 11 (Work)

British Council of Churches, *Work or What?*, CIO 1977.
F. Catherwood, *The Christian in Industrial Society*, Intervarsity Press 1980.
R. Hyman, *Strikes*, Fontana 1977.
Industrial Committee, Church of England, *Work and the Future*, CIO 1979.
C. Jenkins & B. Sherman, *The Collapse of Work*, Eyre Methuen 1979.

Chapter 12 (The Land)

National Farmers' Union – current booklets.
M. Nicholson, *The Environmental Revolution*, Pelican 1972.
P. Singer, *Animal Liberation*, Cape 1976.
J. V. Taylor, *Enough is Enough*, SCM Press 1975.
B. Ward & R. Dubos, *Only One Earth*, Penguin 1972.

Chapter 13 (Doctors and Life)

A. V. Campbell & R. Higgs, *In That Case*, Darton Longman & Todd 1982.
A. S. Duncan & others, *Dictionary of Medical Ethics (Revised)*, Darton Longman & Todd 1981.
B. Häring, *Medical Ethics*, St Paul Publications 1974.
Journal of Medical Ethics Quarterly, Tavistock House, London.
J. Mahoney & others, *Euthanasia and Clinical Practice*, Linacre Centre 1982.
S. Reiser & others, *Ethics in Medicine*, MIT Press 1977.